*AGING IS NOT
FOR SISSIES*

AGING
IS NOT
FOR
SISSIES

by Terry Schuckman

THE WESTMINSTER PRESS
PHILADELPHIA

PUBLISHED BY THE WESTMINSTER PRESS®
PHILADELPHIA, PENNSYLVANIA

PRINTED IN THE UNITED STATES OF AMERICA

Library of Congress Cataloging in Publication Data

Schuckman, Terry.
  Aging is not for sissies.

  Bibliography: p.
  Includes index.
  1. Aged—United States. 2. Aging. I. Title.
HQ1064.U5S38   301.43′5′0973   74-34139
ISBN 0-664-20725-1
ISBN 0-664-24818-7 pbk.

To my Roy

Contents

FOREWORD   11

ACKNOWLEDGMENTS   15

1   *Where in the World Are We?*   17

2   *Keeping Well—Physically*   22

3   *Keeping Well—
     Mentally and Spiritually*   29

4   *How Young Do You Dare to Be?*   37

5   *The Last Enemy*   44

6   *Sense with Dollars*   51

7   *A Place to Live*   60

8   *Something to Get Up For*   69

9   *Just for the Fun of It*   76

10 *School Bells for the White-haired*   83

11 *Putting Old People Power to Work*   90

12 *Some Who Made It—
     Famous and Unfamous*   98

13 *Saying "Yes" to Life*   106

SUGGESTED READING LIST   115

INDEX   119

Foreword

Every one of us ages at exactly the same rate—one day at a time. Yet we have an almost infinite variety of reactions to this aging process. For most of us, no doubt, our dominant response is some kind of attempt to ignore the whole experience—after we reach that favorite birthday where we may like to think of ourselves as "holding" forever and ever. Just as we don't like to consider dying, we also don't like to think of growing old. Yet for each of us, if we live long enough, there are the same necessities to face: the slowing of reflexes, the waning of strength, the fading of memory, the impairment of senses—from what we were at the height of our powers. Yet aging does not mean total collapse. Life can have rich rewards at every age. The loss of some capabilities may be compensated for by growth in other dimensions of mind, spirit, and personality, if we are open to continued growth.

From the very beginning every human being faces countless challenges—physical, mental, emotional. Learning to cope is not an exercise accomplished in a few easy lessons at an early age. It is a lifelong process. The assorted challenges of aging are simply another type of testing, and testing we have to face all through our lives. Terry Schuckman wisely points

out to us that we can learn to cope with these
later-life challenges if we give thought to finding out
what they are before and after we reach them, and if
we develop creative strategies for handling them
stage by stage.

She does not try to lull us into some illusion-filled
forgetfulness of what is happening to us. She gives us
no rose-tinted glasses through which to view the
setting sun. She calls on us to face the realities of the
human condition, but to do so with courage and
imagination. This is an affirmative book that asks us
to accept life, all of life—even growing old. Yet it is
no soft or sentimental plea for resignation. Rather, it
is itself a challenge so to plan our lives as to have
some reasonable chance to grow old with grace and
joy.

Terry Schuckman is a person who, for years, has
practiced what she now preaches. Whether she knew
what she was doing all the time and had some
long-developed strategy, I do not know. Somehow I
doubt it. I am inclined to think that it is simply that
out of the fullness of her own affirmative, ever-
curious, ever-learning spirit there has emerged her
own practical program for how to deal with aging in
a positive way.

As one who has known Terry and Roy Schuckman
for a good quarter century, I have watched with
appreciation the unfolding of her middle-years tal-
ents in painting and writing to complement her
early-years talent in music. I was close to the
Schuckmans in one particularly difficult period when
Terry faced a most grim illness and fought her way
back to full activity and high good spirits. Most of all,

I have observed with admiration the continuing openness and searching of her unfettered mind. There is a special kind of pleasure in being able to testify that the very least which can be said about the one who has written AGING IS NOT FOR SISSIES is that she is no sissy herself. She is, in fact, a wise and witty, courageous and joyful woman who shares, in straightforward simplicity, insights that can be helpful to all who read her words.

LANDRUM R. BOLLING

Landrum R. Bolling, Executive Vice-President of Lilly Endowment, Inc., formerly served for fifteen years as president of Earlham College, Richmond, Indiana.

Acknowledgments

It would seem somehow incomplete if I did not offer thanks and appreciation to those who have helped me along the way. So, though many names are omitted, I should like to mention a few. There is Elton Trueblood, whose vision of his "last third of life" I found most inspiring. I had been working with the subject of aging over many years, but not until Douglas Steere dropped the sentence, "Aging is not for sissies" did I realize that this was the perfect title, binding all my thoughts together. I owe much to Elizabeth Yates, under whose tutelage my thoughts began to jell.

As to the working out, how could I have done without the patient and constant "digging out" of Margaret Jones, head librarian of the Lake Worth library. Or the encouragement of Alice Duxbury, who also helped with research.

Thanks, too, to *Friends Journal* for permission to use two of my meditations; and to Curtis Brown, Ltd., for allowing me to use the lines from Ogden Nash.

Finally, to Frances Wright, who with much diligence and care turned out a beautifully typed manuscript.

Perhaps I should mention Dr. Paul Bauer, my

osteopath, who, when I came to him very tense and out of spirits one morning, said to me: "Remember *you* are not writing this book. It is the work of God, and you just happened to be around when he needed you."

So it is. Each helps the other. And for that too, I am grateful.

CHAPTER 1

Where in the World Are We?

A word spoken in due season,
how good is it!—*Proverbs 15:23*

The due season is now, when we are getting old. And the good word—might it be one we can say to ourselves? It seems to me there are times one has to take up his mirror and look himself squarely in the face. This applies not only to individuals but also to groups. The group that interests me most at the moment is the one usually referred to as "Senior Citizens." In 1958 when I first became interested in the problem of aging there were only nine million people in our country age sixty-five and over. Today there are over twenty-one million. The sheer size of such a group warrants inquiry as to what it should do with itself.

We older people are at the focal point of a special kind of isolationism. Take the phrase "Senior Citizen," for instance. Don't you feel set apart when you hear it? Do you like the term? I, for one, thoroughly despise it. Citizen? Aren't we all—young, middle-aged, and older—*citizens?* And why "Seniors"? Do we refer to young people as "Juniors"? The phrase is far from apt, and was probably thought up by some young, bright person who considers older people crochety, fretful, hard to handle, and generally impossible. The best way to treat this unwieldy, increasingly large group is to tie it up with a nice lavender-and-old-lace ribbon, tag it "Senior Citizens," give the members of it a few privileges, and let them die in peace. If it is your own mother we are talking about, you could send her to Florida to live, where she could sit in the nice sunshine, enjoy the sea breeze, and play cards or whatever she likes to do. In that way you wouldn't have to worry about her. What if she does miss you and the grandchildren? No matter. So it goes. Older people are relegated to the "can't work" pile, to the "always sick" pile, to the "useless" pile—if they aren't totally discarded as being boring, inadequate, old-fashioned, and generally unfit.

I, for one, rebel at this stereotype. In my heart I know I am still an individual without age boundaries. I know also that if I am to hold on to my own concept of myself, my own ego image, I will have to fight for it. I cannot stop to pity myself, or to moan because I cannot face a flight of stairs without trepidation. Of course I understand that there are certain facts of life which I must face, that there are certain limitations which I must set upon myself. But I do not have to accept the limitations set upon me by others, though doctors are a possible exception to this rule. In other words, aging is not for sissies, but for those

willing and able to cope with it. And most of us are
more able than we are willing to admit.

No use to say, "I am not as young as I used to be."
By the same token, you are not as old as you're going
to be. But most of all, you don't have to be a statistic.
You can still be an individual with your own rights
and privileges, just as when you were younger. The
important thing is that we must assess ourselves,
must find out where in the world we are—in relation
to other people, in relation to our children, and in
relation to our jobs.

We have to make a declaration of independence
insofar as we are able. We can do no more. We should
do no less. There are many factors to consider in our
relationships to others if we are to find out where in
the world we are. After considering them, or perhaps
as we consider them, we can establish a new set of
values for ourselves. This is not to say that other
people are not studying us too. Many groups are
involved with the problems of aging. Many colleges
and universities give courses in gerontology and
geriatrics. Government, too—local, state, and federal
—is occupied with the subject. I am not against all
this. I want to benefit from their findings. But they
cannot decide what is good for *you*. *You* must decide
that for yourself, because you are a unique individual, a child of God, bestowed with certain traits and
characteristics that only you possess. There is no one
else in the world quite like you, and only you can see
the world through your own eyes.

But you must be willing to think, to judge, and to
learn. "What, learn, at my age?" Yes! You have a

brain. It is probably just as good as ever, even if, at times, the name of a certain person slips your mind. The thinking faculties are probably the last to deteriorate, especially if you make thinking a habit. So don't let fear, or weakness of body, or anything else interfere with your thinking.

When people say to me: "You are so talented. You seem to have energy for so many things—how old are you anyway?" I answer: "What has age to do with the price of beans? I'm as old as my nose and my two big toes." Surely that is a true statement.

Now to get down to brass tacks, or to use a more modern term—the nitty-gritty. What should you be thinking about to find out where you fit into the world's scheme of things? Well, there are many points to consider. I could use words here such as "We have to understand the physiological, psychological, social, and economic changes that occur with aging, resulting in a certain pattern of living." However, that is not the aim of this book. What I am attempting to do is to discuss with you certain phases of living the older life, things such as health, food, money, housing, perhaps even sex, politics, and death. It is my hope that from our talking things over together, we will come to a new approach to aging.

But this new approach is definitely not for sissies. It requires guts. It requires the courage to face yourself as you are, with the intention of improving yourself. It may even require that you get out of that old, comfortable groove into which you have settled. Of course if you are contented, there is no need to change. But if you are discouraged, lonely, sad, not caring what you eat or when or how, there may be a few suggestions here for you to think about.

I know one man who worked all his life till he was sixty-five. When he retired, he said, "Now I will sit in a rocking chair and rock all day if I want to." He wanted to and he did. A year later they buried him. Other people sit in the antechamber waiting to die. They think their life is over. But I firmly believe that if God kept you going this long, there is a reason, a good reason, for you to go on. I believe that the last third of your life can be useful and fulfilling.

Let me tell you the story of a friend of mine who has just died. She was ninety-three. She had never married. When I last visited her in the Fellowship Community where she lived, in a beautiful room with her own lovely things about her, I noticed again her pink cheeks, unwrinkled face, her shining, bright eyes. And I thought, Behind those eyes there is a remarkable ongoing spirit. Indeed her life was a continuous revelation of that spirit. She had worked among American Indians for many, many years. Her last two days were her only signs of approaching death. I could truthfully say she died young. She had the grit and courage and guts that I am talking about. She was not a sissy. She did not die a thousand deaths before she finally died. You don't have to, either.

CHAPTER 2

Keeping Well— Physically

When you've got your health, you've got just about everything.—*Television commercial*

I wish above all things that thou mayest prosper and be in health.—*III John 2*

Let us consider the body itself first, because it is at hand, it is visible, and it is closer to observation. What do you think of your body? Do you say to it, "I hate the thought of your getting old, because old means something useless and fit to throw away"? How do you think your subconscious regards this statement, so full of dread, if it can understand anything? By this statement, you are already preparing your body for deterioration and paving the way for all sorts of illnesses to find a home, so closely are body and mind intertwined, though for the purpose of this study we are trying to separate their functions.

A sissy says: "I can expect my heart to give out. Everyone's does at my age." And, "Kidneys wear out—they must, after so much activity." Or, "My sister died of cancer, and so will I, probably. It runs in my family." On the other hand, as Harry Hershfield said on a television program, "If it is true that we learn to live by living, then we're that much ahead because we've had a lot of practice."

So let us see what we can do for ourselves—and all through this book we will be "working for ourselves" —with the accent on the positive. Let us first try to understand what this body of ours is—a wonderful grouping of all sorts of cells, each with its own nucleus, protoplasm, cell membrane, and cell wall. The body has millions of these cells, perhaps billions. One group becomes the heart, another the lungs, a third the brain, and so on, all linked together into a glorious whole. And it is this whole, this sense of integrity, that must be held together.

When the body is young, each connection or link is stronger than it needs to be, because a good many strains will come its way. As we grow older these connections become weaker, and since it is inevitable that they do not function as well, aging is a result. The process is uneven. For instance, the brain does not lose its function as fast as some other parts of the body. But uneven or not, there it is. We must accept aging. However, this does not mean that we should not work to prevent it or to slow down the process. One way of preventing it is to see that not too much strain is put on any one link.

How to prevent it? How keep from being attacked by disease? How work to keep the body strong and sure? There are several things we can do.

The first principle, it seems to me, is to keep the body moving. Keep active. Get up from that easy chair. Take that walk. Ride that bicycle. Exercise systematically. Fifteen minutes at each end of the day is not too much. If you move, you can't rust, and the body's joints are constantly being oiled. I know I have to make an effort to sit here at my typewriter. But soon I shall get up and have a coffee break. I can last till then. And afterward I shall return with renewed energy.

I try to use prime time for prime work. For instance, I am tempted to read the morning paper when it comes in. But I can so easily do this later on in the day when my energy is somewhat lower. You, and only you, can decide these matters for yourself. If you think exercise is a bore and a pain and that you can happily do without it, that's fine. Eliminate it. But do get a doctor's opinion first.

As for doctors, they are so expensive these days that I hate to suggest that you see one. But it seems to me important to do so for occasional checkups—to discuss with him your working and sleeping habits, also elimination. This last is neglected by some people and my suggestion to you is to heed the first call immediately—even if it happens to come in the middle of a meal. Don't be squeamish about excusing yourself. If other people fail to understand, that's just too bad. It shouldn't make any difference to you.

As for the doctor, if changes need to be made in your habits, he will tell you so. Go along with him. Should he prescribe medicine that has a bad effect on you, don't just stop taking it. Let him know. Some other medication might serve you better. The doctor can do no more than outline a pattern of living for you. Only you can make it work. If no private doctor is possible for you, then go to a clinic. Often an ailment can show up to a doctor, whereas to you it was not visible.

"My Aunt Gladys fell and broke her hip. I sure wouldn't like that to happen to me. I'd hate to be an invalid." A good many people go through life dreading accidents that might happen in the future. And this is not surprising, for next to cardiovascular disease and cancer, accidents are the greatest threat to the lives of oldsters. But perhaps accidents happen *because* of fear. Face up to the fact that they could happen to you, but also avoid circumstances that are apt to cause them.

I mean, avoid hazards. For instance, don't wax your floors. Don't have small rugs around where they can be tripped over. Look where you're going. Don't reach for things. Walk up close to where they are, or use a wooden reacher with a magnet on the end of it. If you're a man, sit down when putting on your pants. (It's hard to balance on one leg.) Don't load up your stomach with aspirin before breakfast. Have your breakfast first, and then if you need to take aspirin, crush it first. Otherwise you might end up as a friend of mine did, with perforated ulcers. I asked this man why he took two aspirins on an empty stomach every day. His answer: "Because that's when they do me the most good." All right. But know what you're doing to yourself.

Sometimes an older person takes a little longer to find his bearings than a younger person does. Well, here again, don't be a sissy. Realize that getting out of a car takes you a little longer than it used to. And don't be ashamed to take your time. No use to think you might offend someone. The other day, as I came down the stairway from an airplane, the hostess approached me and said, "Can I help you?" "Yes," I

answered. "All I need is a little time." I know that
when someone says to me "Be careful" as I am
getting off the curb to cross the street, I tend to be
annoyed. Why does he think I need help? I'm per-
fectly able to manage. But I smile to myself, accept
the arm, and say nothing. In this way I keep my
dignity and my good nature.

Perhaps the most important thing about the body
in regard to health is to eat enough of the right foods.
A sissy will say: "Why should I bother? I feel O.K., so
my diet must be right." Or: "Toast and tea is good
enough for me. I don't need as much food as I used
to." (An old car needs just as much gas as a new one.)
Or: "It's just too much trouble to cook for one."

You've heard the expression, "We are what we
eat." We are today what we are largely because of
our yesterdays. The older we get, the more yesterdays we have to deal with. In fact, our yesterdays go
back to the time of our nursing, as infants. A woman
I know had a serious operation on her throat when
she was thirty years old. The doctor asked her, "Were
you a bottle baby or did your mother nurse you?" A
little confused by the question, she answered, "My
mother nursed me, but what does that have to do
with now?" His answer, "You would not have been
able to pull through without that extra stamina that
she gave you when you were a baby." Sam Levenson
in his *In One Era and Out of the Other* (p. 121; Simon
& Schuster, 1973) has this to say: "What the child
receives there (at the mother's breast) does not have
to be sterilized, homogenized, or warmed up. It feels
good, smells good, sounds good, even looks good. It is
close to the heart and there are no sharp edges to

hurt him. This is his first taste of love, and it will last a lifetime without artificial preservatives." I mention this for two reasons. One, to show you that the effects of proper eating last a long time; and two, perhaps there is someone you could influence in this regard.

A good diet, although it cannot make up for a lifetime of indiscretion, can improve the body reserves. A sissy will say again: "Why bother? I've come this long way without trouble. I think I can get along without any special effort." O.K. That is, if you want to die by inches. If all you want is a bellyful of food to keep you happy, and you don't care what kind, that's all right. But if you want to be healthy, cut the amounts, yes, but do keep a balance in your daily way of life. This balance should include:

Vegetables—leafy, green, and yellow. One or more servings

Citrus—oranges and grapefruit (or tomatoes, and raw cabbage). One or more servings

Potatoes, other **vegetables,** and **fruits.** Two or more servings

Milk—could be skimmed or made from powdered milk. One pint to one and a half pints

Meat, fish, or chicken. At least one serving

Eggs. Three a week

Bread and cereals. One or both at every meal

Margarine. Two to three tablespoonfuls

Proteins are the building blocks for the body. Some older people think they don't need them anymore, but they do. The diet for oldsters should be high in protein, moderate in carbohydrates (starches, sugars, etc.), rather low in fat, and high in vitamins and minerals. That is, if you want to live out your full life and not get gradually weaker until you die not of old age, but of exhaustion, lack of vitality, and lowered resistance to infection.

Drink, too. No, not liquor—though some doctors may recommend this—but fluids in moderation. If you can't take coffee, drink decaffeinated coffee. Fluids are best taken with meals or just before meals. I myself take decaffeinated coffee at breakfast, tea at lunch and dinner, and milk before retiring. If you like your heaviest meal at lunchtime, eat it then. If you prefer to eat six small meals a day, that's all right too. Do it your way. Cooked vegetables are easier to chew, but don't cook up a whole heap at one time and then expect the goodness in them to last day after day. Cook what you need for the meal. And by the way, in cooking vegetables, cook them in as small amount of water as possible. And if you have any excess, don't pour the liquid down the drain. You need it more than the kitchen sink does. Either drink it, or save it to use as a soup base later. Each meal should have at least one warm food. Don't be a sissy. Take a little time. Put a little love into what you do. Enjoy yourself.

CHAPTER 3

Keeping Well—
Mentally and Spiritually

You are old, Father William, the young man said,
And your hair has become very white;
And yet you incessantly stand on your head.
Do you think, at your age, it is right?
—*Lewis Carroll*, Alice's
Adventures in Wonderland

Do you know people who act as if they were standing
on their heads, or as if their heads were not screwed
on quite right? Some people who look mentally ill
aren't. And some who don't look it at all are. And
many people who worry about losing their minds as
they get older don't. So what is the use of worrying
about it?

But mental health *is* something to think about.
Remember in the previous chapter I said that the
mind and the body cannot really be separated? We
talked about the body by itself for specific reasons.
But you realize that the mind and the emotions do
not exist apart from the body. Indeed, every thought
has a counterpart in the nerve fibers of the brain.
When we are happy or sad or disappointed, these
feelings register in our nervous system, in our glands,
in our bloodstream, in our breathing—and even in

our stomach. (It is good to remember that. For
instance, don't eat when you're angry. The bloodstream can't function.)

Why do I mention this? For two reasons. One is
that older people suddenly thrown out of their
accustomed places—whether it is from a job or a
social situation of some sort where they have been
important—feel that they are useless. This, in turn,
makes them possible candidates for mental trouble.
The second reason is that there is a great need for the
elderly to put their minds in control and not be
dominated by their feelings. After all, the most
powerful drive is the instinct for survival. You must
realize that you have to live through this thing or die.
So react positively, not negatively.

In order for you to understand what it means to
act positively, I will try to give some examples of
negative behavior.

1. There are those people who, when they find
themselves heading into a difficulty, beat a retreat.
Sometimes they "freeze" and become paralyzed, sty-
mied. Or their retreat consists of centering all their
attention on themselves.

2. Others become angry, suspicious, or fearful.
They think the whole world is against them. They
tend to withdraw too, but in a different way. They sit
on the sofa and sulk, bathed in self-pity.

3. Still others, craving solace for some unsatisfied
need, turn to food or "things." Such people tend to
become demanding, insisting that everyone do things
for them. They refuse to accept responsibility.

Now as to positive reactions. Positive people try to
improve their lot, yet appear satisfied to be as they

are. I am thinking of a retired schoolteacher of eighty-five. She has vascular trouble, and is particularly bothered with swelling of the ankles. In addition to this she had viral pneumonia. Do you think she let all this get her down? Not a bit of it! She got rid of the pneumonia right away by refusing to give it a home. This woman is still active in her community. She likes to read, though her eyes have blind spots. Sometimes she takes her book out into the bright sunlight, where she can see better. Her hearing is good, so her children suggested "talking books." But the lady objected. For one thing, she thought that one had to be totally blind to apply for this service. And for another thing, her pride was hurt. Her children arranged it for her, nevertheless. Now she will not be without these books. If you want to know more about talking books, either go to your nearest library or telephone. This woman, at eighty-five, is happy with her lot despite these minor annoyances. She keeps abreast of the news and feels alive.

Another person has locked knees. You would think that with this disability she would find herself in a wheelchair. But not she. Being a woman of spirit, she was determined to drive her own car and she makes it a habit to visit shut-ins regularly.

Another person worked to her seventy-fifth year because she was needed as head of the language department in her school. She decided to quit. At this very time she had a stroke. Not being able to care for herself at home, she entered a good nursing home and waited—but not passively—to see what would come next. As she recovered from her stroke she would use her walker to get about the place, mostly outdoors.

Her recovery was not smooth. She had further small strokes, but each time, as she could, she tried to pull herself out of it. Maybe the other patients considered her snobbish, but she did not mix too much with the depressed or anguished ones. She is waiting for the time when she will be able again to care for herself. She plans at that time to come back to visit the nursing home. In other words, her mind decided that it would work for her physical betterment—and it did.

Mr. H. at eighty-four is a retired Army man. His back gives him trouble. Anyone looking at him might think, He'd be better off in bed. But he doesn't think so. He takes his swim every day and he has an interest in collecting coins—old and new. He found ways to struggle for his betterment.

Mr. S. lived for three years on a houseboat on the Amazon River in South America. He did not even know how to swim, though with crocodiles and alligators in the waters about him, swimming would be of little use. But it does go to show the character of the man. When the foibles of old age came upon him, he resisted them. All these people had spirit!

Organic changes do take place as one grows older. Sometimes there is hardening of the arteries of the brain. Other times there is a narrowing of the arterial tubes because of deposits growing on their walls. And sometimes people are aware of these happenings, and are afraid they themselves will wear out and become senile.

Actually, though, there is reason to believe that your attitude has a great deal to do with how well you can cope with the situation: that psychological changes in old age are as much responsible—or even more so—than organic changes. Recently there have been innumerable instances of recovery through the use of the new methods of physical and mental treatments. So don't go thinking you are about to become senile. True, some people do. Could that be because subconsciously they expect to or want to? Or is it because they cannot seem to hold on to their mental and emotional faculties? I am not saying here that senility is entirely controllable, but I am saying that your intellectual processes, your memory, your interest in maintaining yourself as a clean, lovable person is apt to be in direct relation to your concept of yourself. Make it a healthy one.

If you need help in finding yourself, in every community there is a mental health center where treatment is available. A good many of these are open twenty-four hours a day. Sometimes there is no fee. In other cases, you pay according to your income, starting with $1 per treatment up to possibly $15. And treatments might go on for a period of several months, perhaps twice a week. Anyway, it's something to think about if you need help. But don't give up.

Of the several people mentioned above who behaved positively, four out of the five had religion. This means that they had faith—faith in something larger than themselves, call it what you will: Nature, God, or even Something without a name. Faith is the fundamental, basic element underlying good emotional health. I am thinking of the woman to whom the phrase, "Underneath are the everlasting arms," brings much security. I am also thinking about people who have overcome physical handicaps: the cripple who drives his car and manages his electric fixtures business; the paraplegic, who, without arms or legs, is dictating a book on his experiences in the war; the multiple sclerosis victim who can move only his big toe, but is learning to type on a specially built typewriter; the woman artist with deformed arms who paints with a brush held by her feet. These people are overcoming! And their name is legion. First of all, they have faith in themselves.

Then we need to have faith in others. As we empathize with others we turn the spotlight off ourselves and onto them. This helps in two ways: it helps them improve and grow. And it helps us stop worrying about our own big or little nagging ailments. And we need faith in the desire and capacity of human beings to work out their problems cooperatively. That is the basis of group therapy in which your problem can be talked out. Such a talking out can be both cleansing and healing.

But most of all we need faith in the great Creator of us all, from whom comes help for all occasions. Donald R. P. Marquis put it aptly when he wrote: "All religion, all life, all art, all expression come down to this: to the effort of the human soul to break through its barrier of loneliness, of intolerable loneliness, and make some contact with another seeking soul, or with what all souls seek, which is (by any name) God." (*Chapters for the Orthodox;* Doubleday & Company, 1934.)

In our Quaker Meeting one day, I stood up and shared the following meditation. Let it speak to close this chapter.

We are gathered in Meeting this morning, waiting on God.

What if He doesn't come?

He doesn't have to come. He is already here—everywhere.

In that case, why do I have to come here? Why can't I stay at home and wait upon Him by myself?

You could. But you don't. And even if you did, you could have only the vertical line but would miss the horizontal line, by which you reach out to your fellowman. The inspiration of that fellowship is contagious. It grows as it is multiplied. And the sum is greater than its parts.

What sustains you?

My faith. It lifts me up to receive what there is to receive.

What do you expect?

I expect miracles.

Miracles! Oh, come now! Miracles are hard to come by.

Yes, if you think of miracles in a limited way. But miracles are of all sizes and shapes. A miracle could be a quick shaft of light illuminating what was before a dark, insoluble problem. It could be just a fresh idea. It could be a sense of peace or a moment of sheer, quiet joy. It could be the memory of a child's smile, a bird's song. All these are miracles.

How does one reach out for these?

Through the channel of love.

And is this channel always open? Always free to receive?

No. Frequently it is clogged—clogged with the weeds of distrust, impatience, greed, envy. Sometimes it is filled with despair or futility. But the best clogger of all is hate.

And how does one get rid of hate?

Two things cannot occupy the same thing at the same time. That is a law. Send in love to flush out hate.

Where does one get this love?

From your heart. If you allow it, it will well up from the inner springs of your soul and will reach out to join, through the channel of faith, that greatest source of all love, which is God, and spread out over all men, your brothers.

If sitting here for one hour in the silence can do so much, why is there such sorrow in the world?

Oh, sitting here for one hour once a week won't do it. This is only the big pearl on the endless string of pearls of your days. Each day is its own little pearl of sustenance. Together they form a priceless chain of all of your days. Each day is a day of renewal, of confrontation, of reckoning.

And when we come to the final day of reckoning, at the end of all of our days, will it be easier because of these smaller days of confrontation?

That, my friend, is a question for you, yourself, to answer.

CHAPTER 4

How Young
Do You Dare to Be?

I think the elderly should learn to
liberate themselves.
—*Dr. Sallie Schumacher,*
Modern Maturity,
Feb.–March, 1974

In regard to the various aspects of aging, one of the
subjects people generally shy away from is sex. This
is true whether you are a younger person studying
aging or an older person experiencing aging. I have
noticed repeatedly that on the agenda on aging, the
subject of sex is conspicuously absent. This tends to
make it one of the most basically unexamined subjects. One conference on aging, meeting recently in
Florida, included, for the first time in twenty-six
years, a forum on the subject of "Sex and the Senior
Citizen."

This in spite of the fact that after hunger, sex is
the strongest instinct and one of the greatest human
problems all through life. Persons in their twenties,
thirties, and forties have had their troubles with it.
And when you get to the menopause (and a sem-
blance of the same phenomenon for men in the same

age bracket), you really do not know how to treat the matter.

Part of the reason for this is today's way of advertising, whether on television or elsewhere. The impulse of sex has been blown up into a thousand kinds of displays. If you want to sell an automobile, for instance, just show a lovely young thing, blond preferably, with plenty of cheesecake showing, sitting on top of the car. Or to sell a toothpaste—golf balls—or anything! Our ancestors, on the other hand, did just the opposite. They knew that the species would continue without any help from anyone. And it was considered that to discipline oneself in all matters, particularly in sex matters, was one of the first principles of a civilized society.

Our society is sex saturated. In fact, we are experiencing a sexual revolution. Youth acts as if it had invented sex and, in the name of liberation, is entering into all sorts of experiments. Where sex was once taboo, especially in mixed company, it is now freely and openly discussed by the young. I am all for openness. But I don't know what a slinky female, the latest X-rated movie, a new type of wig, or the latest thing in perfume has to do with sex. Looking sexy has nothing to do with being sexy. You can give a car a wild animal name, but what has that to do with sex? And where does this somehow uncomfortable, dirty feeling creep in? Sex, in its right use, is not dirty. It can be one of the most honest expressions of the very deepest, binding feelings, and it does not belong only to the young.

By the time we reach the age of oldsters, we probably know something about sex. Looking at the first naked man, Adam, and the first naked woman, Eve, we notice that they are conspicuously different, particularly in specific areas. But we know that after God had created them, he saw all, and he pronounced it "very good." If we could only preserve the innocence of that first vision. Adam "knew" Eve. How gently said! And in that "knowing" is the image of a sexual union where two people know each other in the very deepest sense. Their love is bound together more strongly because of their mutually giving act.

How did you first learn about sex? Through friends? Through movies, magazines? From your parents? (I don't know many who did.) In school? Hardly. Sex education is a comparatively new movement, after your time. Or did you learn about it "in the street"?

Why am I going back into all of this? Because your early ideas and your moral concepts regarding sex help to shape your present attitudes. Trying to understand the values of sex, we ask ourselves, What is sex for anyway? First of all, the obvious answer: reproduction. God, or Nature—call it what you will— has made sure that the species will not die out. Secondly, within the sex act may be expressed the most profound, the most revealing, the most selfless, the most binding feeling of devotion and concern between two people. Thirdly, it can be a bringer of sheer joy between two close souls, releasing tensions and restoring bodily harmony between them and also within each individual. And fourthly, this joining together acts as a safeguard, a stabilizing influence over the home, the family, and, through them, the nation.

To illustrate, here are some specific cases:

Case 1. Two people marry—both of them in the twenties—he an administrator and she a nurse. In their first days together, he suggests that they have separate beds, and use sex only for the purpose of having children. Unbelievable? No. Of course that marriage was doomed from the start. Although they had three children and lived together for nearly forty years, it was a most miserable experience, as you can guess. After the death of his wife, the man hired a housekeeper. He was then in his sixties and for the first time in his life he had a satisfying sexual relationship, with this woman, a person of great intelligence and charm. I did not look into their mailbox, so I don't know if they were married. Nor is it my concern. I mention this story because of the great change that took place in the man after he realized that all the purposes of sex must be understood, and that it cannot be limited to procreation alone.

Case 2. This one deals with a woman in her menopause. What looked like a fine marriage on the outside was shaky within. She left her husband and her four children. Later she told me: "He treated me like a prostitute, like a 'thing.' I took it as long as I could." This man had forgotten that loving concern and devotion belong with the sex act.

Case 3. Here is a woman of fifty-five, who had never been married. Her boss, a widower and the father of seven children, liked her very much. They married. What kind of sex life can they have, she being a virgin? She told me about it. "Yes, we had sex. He taught me a lot. We loved each other dearly. Though I had him only five years, they were the most beautiful years of my life, even if his children never accepted me."

Case 4. This woman at sixty-two lost her husband. She told me that she had known only this one man, that their life had been so thoroughly satisfying in every way that now that he was gone she could go on with her work, never missing sex, never even wanting it. She felt fulfilled.

Case 5. Here is a case typical among older people. This man lived alone in a trailer. In the trailer community he found a woman who was compatible with him. He was lonely after the death of his wife and had been living alone for two years. He wanted to be with someone he could love and cherish. Even at age seventy he needed a woman. As he said it, "I'm a sexy septuagenarian." He added, with a twinkle in his eye, "And old ladies need love, too." What of this couple? They would like to marry. If they did, they would lose some of their Social Security, which they could ill afford. So they live together anyhow, their last years brightened by each other. Will society condemn them? It is almost as if the Government would penalize them were they to marry. Yet they could hardly send out cards saying that Henry Davis and Doris Donnelly are pleased to announce that they are living together. Between them they have the wisdom of a hundred and fifty years. And they face the world together bravely, neither one of them a sissy.

Case 6. Two dear friends of mine were married, she
at sixty-eight and he at eighty. They were the two
halves left of a foursome long associated with a
particular college. Of course they came in for a lot of
teasing. "Too bad you *had* to get married, Anne."
And, "Shall we tell you about the birds and the bees,
Tom?" Between them these two had twenty-one
grandchildren. What a beautiful four and a half years
they had together. Neither one would have given it
up for anything. They loved each other dearly and,
far from feeling unfaithful to their former spouses,
they felt, in the cementing of the new relationship,
that they were rounding out the lives of their former
partners.

Was there sex between them? I don't know. They
slept in a double bed, their Quaker marriage certificate above their heads. They were happy together,
this much I do know. Society and particularly religion
still cling to the idea that sex is primarily for the
purpose of reproduction. This would seem to make
sex a "no-no" for oldsters. But the sex urge can
always be there, as long as the people involved want
it. Indeed, a good many women feel a great deal freer
after menopause than before, because unwanted
children are not a possibility.

Individuals vary greatly. Some men are virile in
their seventies. Others are impotent or nearly so in
their fifties. Accommodate yourself to your age.
Oldsters do not necessarily run out of sexual steam.
They may have to change their style a bit and travel
a little more slowly, but what of it?

Grown children may not care for the idea of
Grandma and Grandpa cavorting in bed together. But

in an age when backseat petting and "quickie sex"—furtive and hurried—are common among teen-agers, and when there is flitting about from this partner to that, a stable, loving relationship between two mature individuals is not the worst thing that can happen.

Try entering into sex with a new feeling. Shame is the enemy of sexiness. There is nothing to be ashamed about. You can afford to be open about your bodies and what you are doing. The young and the beautiful do not have all the options on sex. Those who are neither young nor beautiful can be sexually attractive. Be confident. Enjoy!

I am reminded of a story about an older man who was marrying a woman half his age. The doctor warned him: "This can be very strenuous and taxing. Be careful!" To this the man replied: "Well, doc, here's the way I look at it. If it kills her, it kills her."

Come to terms with your own sexuality. Sex is a part of the whole human biology which includes expression of art, music, poetry, and even religion. If your sex life is a delight—and why shouldn't it be now that you are a senior citizen—it can open your eyes to other sides of life which are delightful too. In this matter of all matters, liberate yourself! Don't be a sissy!

CHAPTER 5

The Last Enemy

> **Boast not thyself of to-morrow;**
> **For thou knowest not what a day**
> **may bring forth.**
>
> —*Proverbs 27:1*

If you are a deep-dyed sissy or a sissy of the first water, you will skip this chapter. Who wants to read about death, anyhow? Time enough when we come to it. And why worry about such a morbid subject? There's enough misery in the world as it is.

Behind all this facade of "Too morbid for me," there lies a deep fear and a constant dread. But let me tell you this: You start to die the minute you are born. From the very beginning, cells in your body deteriorate and are cleansed away to be replaced by new ones. There is a cycle of life that starts with your birth. The complete cycle runs like this: birth, adolescence, mating, reproducing, maturing, death. These are basic facts. Death happens to everyone. ("Only not to me. I won't die," say the emotions.)

"But I'm afraid. I don't want to die. I don't even want to *think* about it." Don't you realize that those who conquer this last enemy—and life is a conquering from start to finish—are in much better position to enjoy life? He who fears death is afraid to live. And he who faces death can face life with enthusiasm. We do not have to be concerned with whether or not there is a future. We don't know. But it doesn't matter. Face it! Don't worry about time. Take time before it takes you. And don't kill time. Fill it.

Do you know the story of the man who was asked, as he worked in the field one evening, "What would you do if you knew you were going to die before midnight?" He answered, "I would go right on with my hoeing." But don't you imagine that in spite of this courageous reply, the smell of the earth would become stronger in his nostrils, his sense of the color in the yellow-greening of the sky would become richer, the sounds of evening would fall on a more sensitive ear? Isn't that what would happen? It seems to me that it is so when we accept the fact that death can happen to us—yes, even to you and to me. We can live our allotted time with enthusiasm, and enthusiasm is nothing less than faith in action.

Take the case of Charles Frohman. He had the privilege of sailing the ocean on one of the greatest ships in the world, the *Lusitania*. This big, beautiful ship was torpedoed by a German submarine and many people lost their lives. It was reported by Rita Jolivet, a survivor, that Frohman stood on the deck of the sinking ship and was heard to remark: "Why fear death? Death is only a beautiful adventure." This remains as a tribute to his heroism. He went down with the ship, but he did not permit death to conquer him.

In his book *Death, Be Not Proud* (Harper & Brothers, 1949), John Gunther relates the struggle of his seventeen-year-old son with brain cancer. The son lost both the battle and his life, but he never lost his courage. Death could not conquer him either.

So a good deal depends on attitude. If you face up to death, you can face up to life with more eagerness, with more zest for living. After all, the purpose of life is to live, isn't it? Fully, I mean, and up to the last minute, even if, at the end, you have to give it up after all.

In a recent issue of *Newsweek*, under the heading "Medicine," there was an article called "Can Aging Be Cured?" "We hope," states Dr. Alex Comfort, former director of research in aging at University College, London, "to find a technique for interfering with human aging within the next four or five years—not for stopping the process, but for slowing it down." "Someday," says Dr. Bernard Strehler of the University of Southern California, "we may live almost indefinitely." (What a horrible thought!) I happen to disagree with both these eminent physicians, even though I am a layman and they are medical authorities. It is my idea that it is not how long we live, but how well we live, what we do with the life at hand, that matters. It would seem that nearly everyone wants to live long. But no one wants to become old. Nor do you have to, in one sense, if you live well.

If you look it right in the eye, the fear of death is essentially selfish. We must get rid of that sinking feeling at the pit of the stomach—"What will happen to me after I die?"—and turn to practical ways of handling the days of our years before it is our turn to go the way of all the earth.

Death education is important preparation for living. The first thing is to accept the reality of death as a natural process of life. How awful it would be if death took a holiday and people lived forever and ever. How that would gum up the works!

The second thing is to understand that our own lives—important as they are to us—are part of a much larger whole, a remarkable continuity of life everlasting, a vast flowing stream, who knows how many millions of years old. We have a part in this fabric of life, and as we grow older, we realize the importance of this part we have to play: that we must live our lives as kindly, as creatively, and as vibrantly as possible.

The third thing is to put our affairs in order. This is no small task. It goes without saying that when a person dies, the immediate family is under great strain. The ordinary chores of life become just too much to deal with. So survivors try, as much as possible, to withdraw from the experience. Knowledge of the death is kept from children and young people. But they should be a part of it—we all should be. In that way we are the better prepared when our time comes. A person who has died should not be considered as "passed away," or "gone to rest," or, to a small child, "sleeping." He is dead! There is a finality about that which even a small child can comprehend if you will let him. We should all have a part in the general plan to make dying an actual thing and a natural part of living. How well we die depends in good part on how well we lived.

A good deal of this easement can take place because of what we ourselves have done in preparation. As we grow older, we should gradually diminish our possessions, whittle them down, keeping as little as we possibly can. Then, of course, a will should be drawn. A competent attorney will do this for about thirty dollars. If your will is complicated, that usually means you have more to dispense with and you can afford a higher fee. If you think you have but little, go to a notary public, and before two witnesses, not relatives, state your desires, even if it is just what to do with your body. For instance, if you want to give your eyes to an eye bank, arrange the matter through the local Lions Club. Or if your body is to go to science, indicate that. If burial, where and how. If cremation, say so. Don't leave these things for others to do. It is a strain on them. They will bless you for your thoughtfulness.

I know one couple who have just bought a small plot near their beloved college, where their roots have been for a great part of their lives. When they left the cemetery, each turned to the other with a great sigh. "How good to know that that is taken care of. In this way, we won't be a burden when the time comes." They even bought a small headstone and gave orders for the engraving of their names, leaving out only the dates. Since they live in Florida, they approached the funeral director near the cemetery and gave orders for transportation of the body, what kind of box, etc. This funeral director will contact the Florida director and all will be in order.

Have all your papers in order and in one place. One person I know has a large organizational ledger in which are listed up-to-date records of all assets and liabilities. His wife knows nothing about finances, but all she would have to do in this case is refer to this book. In other words, simplify your life so that you may ease gently into the next experience, whatever it is; the readiness is all.

A word about terminal illness. Were I terminally ill, I would want to know it. Some people do not. Thus, each case has to be handled separately. Perhaps the saddest thing for the dying is the loneliness, when one cannot talk about the things fearful to him that lie ahead. But death should have dignity. And this dignity can be achieved if one understands the various stages of terminal illness: (1) Denial or rejection ("This can't happen to me"); (2) Anger ("This *shouldn't* be happening to me!"); (3) Bargaining ("God, if you get me through this time, I'll do and be anything you want"); (4) Depression ("O God, what am I about to lose?"); and (5) Acceptance ("If it must be, it must be"). This last is a time when communication becomes difficult because of the acceptance, the willingness to be separated from this life. This time can be of the greatest importance, when just closeness, sitting by in silence and holding the hand is all that is required. Dr. Elisabeth Kübler-Ross in her book *On Death and Dying*, pp. 34–121 (The Macmillan Company, 1970), deals very fully with the subject of terminal illness.

One cannot accept life without knowing that it must end. Having prepared for the ending somehow gives one a sense of freedom and release. It was François de Salignac de La Mothe-Fénelon who wrote, "There were some who said that a man at the

point of death was more free than all others, because
death breaks every bond, and over the dead the
united world has no power."

This freedom means that we can forget about it
and go about the business of living with greater joy,
appreciating nature—trees, mountains, the sea—and
take greater delight in friendship. It gives us an
opportunity to love and cherish life the more because
we realize that life and death are but opposite sides
of the same coin, each necessary to the other.

Overcoming! That is the word. Because life and
death are concerned with the eternal process of
becoming, the last effort must be one of overcoming.
Perhaps it is not quite right to call death an enemy,
but that the fear of it must be overcome is more than
relevant—it is essential. Woven into life is all that is
rich, noble, and triumphant. And woven into death is
also all that is rich, noble, and triumphant. Because
older people are sitting in the vestibule at the very
edge where life and death meet does not mean that
they must sit in fear and wait for the inevitable.
Inevitable? Yes. But fear? No! Once one's attitude is
clear and confident, once one sees one's place in the
eternal scheme of things, once one's affairs are in
order—one can let go and live. And live to the fullest
extent, with confidence and the fullness of joy!

CHAPTER 6

Sense with Dollars

O money, money, money, I am not necessarily
one of those who think thee holy,
But I often stop to wonder how thou canst go
out so fast when thou comest in so slowly.
—From "Hymn to the Thing That Makes the Wolf
Go," by Ogden Nash. Copyright © 1934 by Ogden
Nash. Reprinted by permission of Curtis Brown,
Ltd.

"Okay. So I've reached retirement age after scraping
and saving all my life." "For what?" you ask. "For a
rainy day! Well, the rainy day is now. And my
umbrella is full of holes. How shall I spend wisely
what money I have now?"

You have heard folks talk like this. It is well to
remember the proverb, "A fool and his money are
soon parted." We older folks do not consider ourselves
to be fools. But perhaps we have been just a little
careless or thoughtless in the handling of money
matters. Not so many years ago a New York department store, perhaps the largest such store in the
world, had as its slogan: "It's smart to be thrifty."
Being thrifty at that time seemed like a far-out idea.
Today, in a time when we see our resources slipping
away—not only on a national scale but on a world-
wide scale—thrift is a must. Have you thought how
much of a bite rampant inflation takes out of your

dollar? It affects your money in the bank, your life insurance, your annuities. So take stock of where you are. It might be a good idea to make a picture of the state of your finances. This is called a balance sheet, showing what you own (assets) and what you owe (liabilities). Ask your bank for one of these balance-sheet forms. (Banks use them when people come to borrow money.)

Do you have a bank? I know a man who always came to pay his rent, $150 a month, in cash. When the landlord suggested he would be glad to accept a check, the man said: "Never use 'em. What money we have we spend. Wouldn't know how to do it any other way." This man needs educating. He should know that banks can be helpful.

If you have never used a bank, you should know that there are several different kinds. To save, choose one that has the word "Savings" in its name. It usually pays a somewhat higher interest. Should you need some cash before the interest period ends, don't draw out of your savings account but borrow from the bank. Reason? You will be more apt to pay back to the bank what you owe rather than to yourself. As for checking, a good many banks permit senior citizens to have checking accounts free.

I will try to give you some information on being thrifty. Remember: I don't know all the answers. These are just suggestions. Use them if they apply in your case.

CREDIT CARDS. These are days of easy credit. Everyone wants to sell us goods and services. It is sometimes hard to know where the services begin and the goods end. A credit card can be a blessing, if wisely used. But get the habit of feeling that in using it, you are spending money. Also realize that it can be expensive. Since we oldsters have a more or less fixed income, we have to discipline ourselves in our buying, and become good shoppers. This is something that can be learned. If you should lose your credit card or have it stolen, it can cost you money, especially if you don't report it right away. Pay your credit bills on time (the "fly now—pay later" has come home to roost). If you don't pay on time, you are charged interest. By the way, you don't need more than one or two credit cards. That should be enough. Destroy all the others, and also any that might come unasked for in the mail.

BUYING A CAR. This is the time to think small! (Remember the gas shortage.) Don't buy fancy gadgets. A radio is a must. And air conditioning, if you are going to a warm climate. And that's *all.* A four-door car is easier for the little lady (those big two-door panels can be so heavy). When to buy it? The best time is before you actually need it. That gives you time to look around. This could be at summer's end. Or late in the fall after the new models come in. Another good time is in the winter, when car dealers are usually sitting around twiddling their thumbs. Of course, if you come across a sale, take advantage of it. Remember that your car starts to depreciate as soon as it leaves the salesroom. So take good care of it. Use the best engine oil you can buy. Keep the car in good repair. And remember that whitewalled tires don't ride any better than the other kind.

STOCK MARKET. With uncertainty as consistent as this has been of late, who can advise? But if you must play Wall Street, investigate before you invest. If you have a weak heart that goes thumpety-thump every time the market loses a point, then this area is not for you. On the other hand, if money interests you, and part of the fun of your day is to go downtown and watch the big board, and *if* you can afford to take a loss, do it. It's your choice.

SUPERMARKET. Everyone has to shop for food. Make it a practice, if you can, to go only once a week. In the food area, more money can slip through your fingers than is usually realized. Make a list, take it with you, and stick to it. Buy foods that will sustain you. No junk foods (sweets, cookies, pies, potato chips, soft drinks, etc.). Frozen orange juice is good, but if you prefer to squeeze your own, that's fine, but you should know that it usually costs a bit more. Have an emergency shelf that will stand you in good stead if there's bad weather on your regular shopping day, or if you're not quite up to shopping, or if a guest drops in. You can cut your milk bill by using dry milk. Several good brands are on the market. You don't like the taste of it? You'd be surprised how fast you can learn to like it, if it is well mixed. Use your blender, or even an eggbeater.

Don't buy on impulse. If meat is high, then skip meat and buy fish. You don't care for fish? Cheese will do for protein, or lentils, or soybeans, or nuts, or eggs. And remember: brown eggs are just as nutritious as white ones.

Buy what is in season, if at all possible. And keep

away from luxury foods. Use extenders as little as
you can. They help fill you up but not with what
counts.

Watch the person doing the checking out. Checkers
are only human and can make mistakes. Carry a
rollaway, folding cart in your car. It can save you
energy.

INCOME TAXES. You know the two things in life
that are sure: death and taxes. A cliché? So what? A
cliché gets that way because it's often true. The
Federal Government and three quarters of the states
levy an income tax. The data you supply is put on
special forms called tax returns. If you don't receive
the forms, that's no excuse. If you don't keep
accurate records, that's no excuse. Severe penalties
are exacted if you don't pay.

The Internal Revenue Service (IRS) is part of the
Treasury Department. Each city has its own IRS
Division and it can be reached by telephone. Or,
better still, go there in person. They will be glad to
help you understand the tax laws, and answer all
your questions. Many, many persons pay too much
because they fail to understand these laws. So become familiar with them. They change from year to
year, so it is a help to have a current booklet on tax
matters, which is inexpensive. Or if you are still on a
job, your company will get this information for you
free.

You must understand that IRS personnel will not
fill out your return for you, but they can help. They
will assign you a special identification number if you
need it. If you have trouble filling out your tax

return, get an accountant to do it. This is not as expensive as you might think. It can cost from twenty to fifty dollars or more, depending on how involved your form is. But it's worth it. How do you find a good accountant? The same way you find a doctor, a lawyer, or a repairman. Ask your friends.

LAWYERS. A good lawyer is a must. He can become your confidential friend. But he must be someone you like and can trust. If you don't have one, get one. In any case, you will need him to make out that will, remember? To find a lawyer, look under the appropriate listing in the Yellow Pages. The ad in my book says half-hour visits can be arranged for a fee that any person can afford. (This is often a public service of the county Bar Association.)

A FEW GENERAL TIPS. Usually with a man and wife, one of the two handles money better. Let whichever one is more able do it.

Buy good appliances in the first place. Hold on to the warranty or guarantee.

If you have air conditioning, keep the sun out as much as possible.

Learn to sew. Clothes are getting higher and higher in price.

Keep your pleasures simple.

When having the main meal out, plan to do it at lunchtime. It's less expensive.

Shop during a store's slack hours. You will get better buys and more attention.

Buy a small broiler to use instead of using the large oven.

Don't go overboard on cosmetics.

Gifts for grandchildren? This is where you can waste your money. Most of the expensive gifts are unsuitable. Give the children something to work with.

Two oldsters can live together more cheaply than one plus one. But they must be compatible, perhaps sharing a common living room, and leaving one bedroom each for total privacy.

Know your rights when you buy on time. New York State Banking Department, 100 Church Street, New York, N.Y. 10007, will send you a booklet about this.

If you are hiring a person to do your tax return, have all the papers ready. (Check stubs, sales tickets, other memos.) This will save you time and money.

SUPPOSE YOU ARE POOR. Suppose you don't have investments, insurance, pensions, bank accounts, charge plates, credit cards, and all the rest. Suppose you are just plain poor and need help. I dislike that word "poor." I wish I could find another one—perhaps "low-income level" or "without sufficient funds." But that's just hedging. Everyone knows what is meant by the word "poor." Many of us have been poor at some time. When I begin to feel poor I usually go and buy something extravagant—like the time I didn't have enough for the week's food, and I went out and bought six French china plates—Quimpères, they were called. Oh, that made me feel great! It took away that dreary feeling of just not having enough. Now every time I look at those hand-painted plates, I feel good.

But to get down to brass tacks. There are food stamps to be had. (Call your Family Service or the

State Welfare Department to find out where and how stamps can be obtained.) Then there are meals-on-wheels programs in some communities. In this case, cooked food is usually brought to the home. Another program is communal meals, where a hot meal is served each day, with transportation to take you there, usually to a central place, a school for instance.

If you are receiving Social Security and it is not enough, there is something called Social Security Supplement. This provides, too, for Medicare and Medicaid. And in some cases doctors' bills and even drugs are paid for. Ask at the Social Security office nearest you.

There is Lift Line, a transportation help for the elderly. And also Home Nursing Service. Another facility called Homemaker Service is available to anyone at a price the individual can afford to pay. Persons come in for part of a day, or part of a week, to do light housekeeping.

Under the CHEER program in Florida there is a project to help you stay or become physically fit. It is called Physical Relaxation for Older Persons. (By the way, that word CHEER stands for *C*enter for the *H*abilitation and *E*ducation of the *E*lderly and *R*etired.) I mention this because in your community there must be something of the sort. It's free, and when you are physically fit you are better able to handle your problems, whatever they may be— money or anything else.

In other words, do something for yourself. Don't be a sissy. Don't crawl under a rock. Get into the action. Use your imagination. Whatever your station in life, whatever your needs, whether you are in the money or not, there is some way for you to get help. All that is needed is for you to want it and to go after it.

And, bless you!

CHAPTER 7

A Place to Live

> **Yea, the sparrow hath found a house,**
> **And the swallow a nest for herself.**
> —*Psalm 84:3*

> **You are a king by your own fireside,**
> **as much as any monarch in his throne.**
> —*Cervantes*

Are you in a bind as far as housing is concerned? Most older people are, because as their Social Security benefits go up, so does the rent. There seems to be very little we can do about our greatest enemy—runaway inflation.

Now, it is true that a good many older people own their own homes. By this time, the mortgage is probably paid and the children have left home. And what do two old people want with a big house? Or perhaps you are alone, in which case the sounds seem even worse in the echoing rooms. Where to go and what to do?

When you think of selling and going somewhere else, you have to choose that somewhere, *before* you sell. If you don't, you might feel somehow disconnected. People who can afford it travel to places where they would like to live, and give it a try. If it's Florida, you cannot judge by the many winter vacations you have enjoyed there, because Florida, on a year-round basis, is something else again. For instance, the summers may not be hotter than where you are now, but they last from April through October—a good six months. Each locality has its own special pros and cons, its own special flavor, be it Arizona, or California, or wherever. So try it out first. Expensive? Unreasonable? Maybe. But it would be worse to make a mistake. Moving can be traumatic. In any case, moving costs a lot of money. Make sure it's worth it.

Let's take a sample case. You now live in Michigan and would like to move to Florida. Let's assume you have considered all the angles concerning such a move, and you have decided on a condominium. Now you are ready to sell your house. It's a good, two-story, two-bathroom house, complete with attic, basement, and garage. Not new—you have lived in it for twenty years. The place in Florida is small, only two bedrooms and one bath. No garage. No basement. Very limited storage space.

Shall you get an agent to sell your house for you? If you do get a realtor, make some arrangement with him so that you are permitted to sell it yourself, if occasion warrants. Price the house somewhat higher than it's worth. (People like to bargain.) Clean it up. Fix leaky faucets, creaky steps, broken doorknobs, etc. And paint the outside. (Not the inside—people like to choose their own colors.) Shrubbery and grass should look well cared for.

When you show the house, have as few people in it as possible. This makes it easier for potential buyers to imagine themselves living in it. Don't oversell.

Keep quiet. It might be a good idea to list some statements about the house on a sheet of paper and give a copy to the potential buyer as he leaves. He is probably looking at other places too. This fact sheet will remind him of details about your house, how much it costs to heat, what the taxes are, whether there are screens and storm windows, how near to schools, shopping, and even a hospital. The prospective buyer might like to know how near it is to the church of his choice, and whether there's a bus route nearby. People will appreciate your thoughtfulness, and your house will seem "special."

Late spring and early fall are good times to sell a house. But don't expect that the first person who sees it will buy it. We had thirty people come before we sold our house, but those who bought it are happy and satisfied.

Now comes the hard part. You are moving into a small place. You will have to shed many things. One doesn't realize how precious one's possessions are until one is about to part with them. But this parting is a must. It hurts. We had an auctioneer come in. If you do this, be sure not to be at home at the time. It's a dreadful experience.

Because we were moving to Florida we could not take some of our large, heavy pieces. Besides, this dark furniture looked fine in our old house but would never do for the South. Some people take nothing and start afresh when they get to the new place. Others take some things, as we did. But there is the expense of carting them down, and then finally having to give them up after all. You just have no idea how little it takes to furnish a small place. Of course, take the

dear things that are very close to your heart—but
don't take too many.

As for buying a new place, what kind will you buy?
You have cash in hand, more than enough to pay for
the house outright. But don't. Get a mortgage. In
case of resale, this is important. And what kind of
house will it be? A private home? A condominium,
either garden-type or hi-rise? A cooperative? Or
perhaps you are thinking of a mobile home. In
Florida, for instance, 25 percent of the living is done
in trailers. Whatever the kind, choose a place where
you will be comfortable, among people more or less
like yourself. What attracted me first to the place we
live in was the sight of fresh, clean clothes hanging
out on the lines; concealed, of course, but not completely. I said to myself, I like people who like clothes
hanging out in the sun to dry. Besides, I liked the
sound of the name, Cresthaven Villas. Each villa,
though attached to its neighbor, boasted its own
pretty (though to me, unfamiliar) pink and red
flowers. In front of the villa that we were considering
stood a lovely yellow hibiscus tree. In every direction
there was something peaceful and beautiful to be-
hold, all freshly trimmed and manicured. Much of the
sky showed, the blue peeking through the fluffy white
clouds. I thought to myself, This is for me. However,
I wanted to see what kind of people lived here. So we
meandered over to the pool, a stone's throw away,
and we saw the people, and the beautiful clubhouse.
From there we went to the sales office, where, believe
it or not, we were told to go look at some other places
just to make sure we wanted to live here. We did go
and we did look, but always returned to Cresthaven.

And therein lies the success of this particular condominium community in West Palm Beach.

Some people prefer hi-rises. To others a hi-rise would not be acceptable. A one-story, garden-type with no steps to climb, and no elevators to wait for, is for them much more desirable. They feel more "individual" than in a large complex. But you are the chooser. Make your own decision.

Find a developer who stays with the project. Understand what the term "maintenance-free living" really means. Does it apply only to the outdoors? Just what does it include? Examine the recreation facilities. Find out whether the bus service really works, and how often. Are pets allowed? What restrictions are there in connection with resale? Buying a house used to be a big deal, but these days things are more fluid. People find that if things do not suit them, it is possible to change. Make sure that you understand all the terms of your contract, which, we hope, is written in good English—not legal verbiage —so anyone who reads it can understand. (Sometimes people are asked to pay for parking space that they thought they were getting in the basic price.) Make sure everything is clear. And never sign any papers until you have read them carefully—yes, even the fine print.

Wherever you buy, realize that the house in a particular community, in a particular place, with certain physical equipment, is not the whole story. It must be related to your health, your recreational needs, your job, if any. Once you have gotten over the hurdles of selling your old house, moving, parting with your possessions, and settling in the new place, a

certain amount of adjusting is to be expected. As we
said in the beginning, aging is not for sissies. It is
painful to move, but the pain can be overcome. What
hurt at the time of moving becomes only a faint
memory after two years.

We have been talking about one segment of older
people, the ones who can afford to pick up and move,
and who have the energy and the finances to do so.
But housing is a much bigger problem than that. If
we could solve the problem of housing, we would be a
long way toward solving other problems connected
with aging. For housing, next to health, is probably
the most important factor in the life of an older
person. Why? Because an older person spends a good
deal of time in his own home. Every person is entitled
to a home that is decent, a good place in which to live.
He has to feel secure in it. These days, when older
people—and others—feel insecure in the streets,
perhaps the home is more important than ever
before.

What about being lonely? Loneliness is the number
one killer. In some of the houses put up by the
government, buzz buttons are put in for the person
living alone, so that he can get help if needed. Also a
buddy telephoning system is arranged to keep daily
check. Ideally, in the eight-unit, small-housing facilities being built in some places, there is supervision by
a group of nurses and social workers. The older
person should be able to walk to the library, to a
restaurant, perhaps to a movie house, certainly to a
drugstore or to a health clinic. Access to a church
brings satisfaction to many people.

Suppose you are considering a retirement home.

There are many good ones all across the country,
some elegant, some plain, some church-sponsored,
others independent. They are of all different kinds
and sizes. If you would like to live in one, go and visit.
Talk to the residents. Have an occasional meal there.
In this way you will find out what the score is. Some
people arrange to give all their money to such an
institution and then live there for the remainder of
their days. If that suits you, do it.

If you are a candidate for a nursing home, you
yourself probably cannot go to look at it. But have
the relative or friend or social worker who does go for
you look at several homes, and not at show time—
Open House, for instance, when everything is made
to look rosy—but at other, unexpected times. Have
your friend look into the kitchen, talk to the patients
in the rooms and in the halls, and note their reactions.
Some nursing homes are good and others do not have
satisfactory ratings. In any case, consider that entering a nursing home is a temporary thing and
expect that you will one day become well enough to
be on your own. Act with confidence even though you
do not feel quite confident. Accept it as a crutch for
the moment.

Accepting crutches reminds me of a man who had
trouble walking. He was living at home, with a
visiting nurse coming in regularly. When she suggested a walking stick, he said: "Oh, no. I can't think
of myself as depending on a stick." When he was
ready for the stick, he found that it wasn't enough
and that he needed a walker instead. Again he
rebelled. "Me? A walker? Ridiculous! What will
people think?" So again he refused help. When he was

ready to accept the walker, he found he needed a wheelchair. "A wheelchair! The badge of the permanent invalid. Not me!" You know the rest. When he was ready to accept the wheelchair, he had to take to his bed, from which he never rose. So accept the appliance, whatever it is, for the time you need it. Accept it with dignity and courage. When you have finished with it, discard it.

Truly, a man's house is his castle. Whether it is a mansion, a small apartment, a tiny room, or even a cave, fill it with love. It is the place where you have your being. Make your house a home, a place where not only your problems but your satisfactions are bound together. Housing is a big consideration. It deals with your need for independence, your need for security, your need for knowing who and what and where you are, and your need for well-being. A house is more than just a shelter where you can keep out of the rain and the cold. It is more than a list of conveniences like a nonskid bathtub or a ramp for easily getting in or out.

Many organizations are working for you in respect to housing. There are unions, church groups, associations of homes for the aged, nursing homes, boarding homes, etc. People who are working for you include doctors and nurses, dietitians, social workers, and ministers. But the one person who must do most of the work, be it in the housing area or any other, is yourself. Put your best foot forward, and pretty soon the other foot will come up to meet it. Show some courage, some vigor (even though you don't feel any), some energy (even if you don't have much). Using your independence, such as it is, will bring you more independence. You don't have to believe that, but the least you can do is try. You have nothing to lose but continuing and downgrading disability. Good housing is primary to the good life. Aspire to it! Get it for yourself. Perhaps then you can help others get it too.

CHAPTER 8

Something to Get Up For

> **Work, for the night is coming,**
> **When man works no more.**
> *—Annie L. Coghill*

"I'll be sixty-five next month and I guess I'll have to quit my job. Why quit? Who'll make me?" Well, you know very well who: your boss, or the company, or the school system, or the factory—they decide when you should go.

"But I feel fine. And I'm able to do the job. I *should*. I've been at it for nearly forty years. I've still got a lot of work left in me."

No use to fight City Hall. You'll get your gold watch and the fine dinner, and out you'll go.

Some companies like it that way. Actually they can get a younger person to take your place for much less than they are paying you. Besides, you've got to make room for those younger people. You've heard all the reasons.

A good many people feel there's something wrong about that. To quote *Newsweek* of May 27, 1974:

> In the past five years, the Labor Department has filed 200 suits to enforce the Age Discrimination in Employ-

ment Act, charging various companies with unfairly treating employees in the 40–65 age group; it has won many of the suits, but all were very small. Last week, however, Labor attorneys announced their biggest victory to date. In a negotiated settlement, Standard Oil of California agreed to pay $2 million in back pay to 160 older workers it had fired and to rehire 120 of them.

It must be a terrible shock for a person who has worked all his life to find himself suddenly without a job—unwanted and unneeded. However, I heard one man, a teacher, say he never felt so free as he did after he retired. He could now criticize and say whatever was on his mind without having to stop and think, What will the system think about this?

Don't let retirement come as a shock. The trick is to prepare for this eventuality *before* it happens to you, and while you're still young. The only trouble is that young people do not care to think about this matter at all. They find it depressing to realize that they will ever grow old. But many people, when they finally get to be senior citizens, don't feel old at all, inside. At a twenty-year college reunion, Jane might say: "My, hasn't Mary grown old! But not me—I feel young!" She doesn't know that Mary feels the same way about her.

To get back to the subject of work, why work when you can relax and take it easy? Do people work just to make money? Of course some have to. But there are other reasons for working: to meet people, to feel needed, to contribute something worthwhile to life, to keep young, to stay in the mainstream. Some educators say that this mainstream is now polluted; best to stay out of it. But if that is true, we should find a way to un-pollute it.

Work is important. A man was given a brain and a body, and he must use them. But the body begins to wear out, and aging begins to take over. Aging, after all, is a process of disengagement. And what is disengagement if it is not release from activity? But since aging is a *process* and not an on-the-spot kind of thing, it must be something that takes time. So release should be gradual. Doing nothing can be enjoyable for a time. But if a man is smart, he will soon attach himself, for pay or for no pay, to something else to keep him busy. And if he is *very* smart, he will have arranged for this beforehand, while he is still working.

If you have a latent hobby, develop it *now*. Turn that extra room off the garage into a workshop. Enroll in a high school woodworking class. Or get out that camera. This is a kind of insurance.

What I've said about men applies to women too. Indeed, women have an extra job to do: when their husbands quit working, these older women have to deal with their husbands' retirement problems. It becomes a whole new ball game. A woman who is a good cook can teach teen-agers at the "Y" how to cook well. Or she could market her fine jams and jellies. Some women can sew well, and have unusual ideas about making aprons, or pants suits, or whatever. Share these ideas. There is a real boom in the sewing market.

But what if you're an old person in a home for the aged? I read about such a home in New Jersey where the average age is eighty-three! A coordinated plan was worked out between the home and a service organization which was doing work on a subcontract basis. The work involved very simple operations, like slipping small pencils into compasses and assembling kits for school use. The residents work three hours a day, four days a week, each person according to his physical ability. If one of them happens to be in bed one day, the work is brought to him. It is useful work, not busywork. Everyone is paid. Not much, but it *is* pay. Better by far than lying in bed, worrying about yourself. The unofficial supervisor of this project is a man of ninety-three! He enjoys his work and says, "I do whatever I am given to do. At my age I don't complain."

During the war, a woman of fifty applied to the Red Cross as a recreation worker. She was interviewed by a special committee member, who said to her, "I am your age, but I could never do such work." To that came the reply: "Am I correct in assuming that you are not a working woman? I, on the other hand, am work-oriented. I've worked all my life." She was accepted.

Another woman came home from serious brain surgery. She knew she would be a long time getting well. It made her nervous to visit with people, but she wanted to keep herself occupied. A program was arranged by the local cancer clinic for her to roll bandages. Work can be a great healer. It can keep you from anxiety about your physical condition. It helps you remember who and what and where you are. Don't believe the great lie: "You belong on the shelf!" Nobody can put you on the shelf but yourself, except if you're a sissy. Don't wait for the world to come to you. You have to ask for what you want.

It is perhaps startling to see so many people over

sixty out job-hunting. But there are jobs galore for those three score or more. The thing is to find them. CHEER, previously mentioned, has a listing of job opportunities where employers accept mature workers (age sixty plus). One such person got a job managing a concession stand at the park zoo. She pulled it out of the red, and later said, "That was the most rewarding and challenging job I've ever had." Another person, who hadn't worked for several years but was beginning to feel the squeeze of inflation, found a part-time job as bookkeeper at a local drugstore.

If you have four hours a week to spend, use it to help with the answering service. In our town it is called Crisis Line. After a training period, you can be of service to people by referring them to various agencies where they can get help. No pay, but what a great satisfaction!

Here are some government programs that may interest you. Some are for pay, and some not:

FOSTER GRANDPARENTS. This program gives low-income adults opportunity to work closely and regularly with neglected children in institutions, correction homes, hospitals, schools for the mentally or physically disabled. They work two hours a day, five days a week—for pay. They give the children love and continuing attention. The children give them much in return.

RSVP. (*Retired Senior Volunteer Program.*) This grew out of the Foster Grandparents project. If your income exceeds a certain amount, there is no pay but the work is done on a volunteer basis, though your carfare is paid. Volunteers in this program work in welfare offices, recreation centers, schools, day-care centers. Workers are very much in demand. You won't be turned away.

VISTA. (*Volunteers In Service To America.*) Persons live and work among the poor in the United States, Puerto Rico, and the Virgin Islands. There is a training period of from four to six weeks. Service is for one year—in ghettos, rural poverty areas, etc.

PEACE CORPS. After a training period, these volunteers work abroad in many countries, serving two years. Transportation is paid to the training stations, and to and from the overseas assignments. There is a basic pay, and a readjustment allowance of $75 when the work is over. Persons with basic skills are preferred. Although this is an advantage to the older volunteers, age is not enough. What is needed is an outgoing person with a warm heart. Whereas age is no barrier, health must be good. One man of ninety-three was sent to South America to teach the almost lost art of bricklaying by hand, a skill he had been practicing for eighty years.

SCORE. (*Service Corps Of Retired Executives.*) This is a service in which business men and women from many fields where they have been executives, can act as counselors and advisers.

PROJECT GREEN THUMB. If you like working outdoors with conservation, farming, or parks, this is for you. The main concern of the project is to beautify and develop the earth.

With so many opportunities to choose from, don't say, "What is there to get up for?" There's plenty of work still to be done, if you are able. And when you do it, put your very best into it.

Here is one of my favorite poems, and although it refers to "things" the same principle applies to the quality of all good work.

I AM ONLY A PIECE OF WORK

After I leave your hands
You may never see me again. People
Looking at me, however, will see
You and, so far as they are concerned,
I'll be you. Put into me your best
So that I may speak to all who see me
And tell them of the master workman who
Wrought me. Say to them through me,
"I know what good work is." If I am shabby
And poorly made, I will get into bad company;
Then show through me your joy in what you do,
So that I may go the way of all good work,
Announcing wherever I go that I
Stand for a
Workman that needeth not to be
Ashamed.

—*William C. Smith*

CHAPTER 9

Just for the Fun of It

> If I am not for myself, who will be?
> But if I am only for myself, what am I?
> —*Rabbi Hillel*

> By labor Wisdom gives poignancy to pleasure,
> and by pleasure she restores vigor to labor.
> —*Fénelon, in* Télémaque

Can you imagine a doctor on his time off picking up his violin case and, choosing the quietest place in the hospital, the morgue (!), playing there for over an hour?

Can you imagine a cleaning woman who works six days a week spending her Sundays visiting the sick in the hospital? I asked her, "Do you know that many sick people?" And she said, "No, but I go to the desk and ask if there's anyone who wants to be read to, or someone I can do an errand for, or someone who needs to be fed."

What do these two people, the physician and the housecleaning woman, have in common? They are using their leisure hours for their own satisfaction— to do that which pleases them most. Nobody tells them they have to do this or that. It is their own choice, made freely, for their own relaxation and refreshment.

Recreation is a part of life for everyone, regardless of age. But in the last third of your life it is especially important. It can make valuable contributions to your life by enlarging and increasing your interests. It gives you an opportunity to express yourself. It permits you to get involved with other people who have the same likes.

Now, what do you like to do? You have many choices—even the choice to do nothing at all! That may be all right for a short time, but in the long run it brings you nothing but ashes, and eventually death.

A friend writes me: "I am really glad to be retiring (never thought I'd be able to say that!). The disturbing thing is that *everybody* asks me, 'Now that you are retiring, what are you going to do?' I'm *expected* to say that I'm going to travel, or I'm going to write a book. What else does an alleged 'Professor' *do?* So they are all somewhat taken aback when I say that I'm going to clean out my basement! First things first! Travel may come later, if I can figure out whether I can afford it!"

So what will you do with your time, now that you have lots of it? If you like to play games, you have a whole host to choose from. There are the sit-down games like cards, word games, brainteasers, and others. If you like to throw paint on a canvas or work with ceramics, you can do that. The larger movement activities are more appealing to some. A former plastic surgeon who lived in what he calls "a quaint part of New York City"—Park Avenue—and is now living in Florida, plays tennis at least three times a week. An ex-policeman excels at shuffleboard. There's swimming and dancing. You should see these

older people in their fancy, colorful skirts—square
dancing. The steps are slower, but how they enjoy it.
There's also folk dancing, which is now staging a
comeback. Or there is skating, or really anything you
like. I still have in memory the picture of a bald-
headed man, whizzing by me on the sidewalk, when I
was a child. "Skating! Why, that man must be at
least seventy," I exclaimed. "He's eighty, but he goes
like sixty!" came the reply.

Then there's music: playing in an orchestra, or
singing in a choral group or barbershop quartet. I
heard one on television yesterday that was simply
delightful. It was on a program called "Grandpeople"
(instead of "Senior Citizens") and it featured this
quartet, the members of which were fifty-three,
fifty-eight, sixty-two, and eighty years of age. They
wore the traditional straw hats, and sang the old
chestnuts, such as "When You Wore a Tulip," "I
Want a Girl Just like the Girl," "Old Gray Bonnet,"
and "Goodbye, My Coney Island Baby." I don't know
who had more fun—they doing it, or I listening.

There is also little theater. As a senior citizen (I
still don't like the term) I had the thrilling experience
of appearing as the matchmaker in the musical
Fiddler on the Roof. It was in Richmond, Indiana,
where one of the finest little theaters in the country
boasts the leadership of a genius, Dr. Norbert Silbiger, after whom the theater is named. The interest-
ing part of this story is that I never forgot a line, nor
did the person, over seventy, who played Tevye. And
the director was himself near his middle seventies.
The production remains in my memory as one of the

liveliest, most brilliant folk musicals of all time. Who dares say the word "old"?

But if acting is not your cup of tea, there are many other things you can do to amuse yourself. If you get a book out of the library on recreation activities, you will find a whole list of things you may want to look into, including things of the mind such as discussion groups (current events) or the Great Books project (a group study of good and significant literature).

All the aforementioned are fun things that can amuse you and help you to pass the time in a worthy way. If recreation is anything, it is a wholesome program that stimulates physical and mental health. It can increase your life expectancy and give you a feeling of "belonging."

However, I am thinking of something that is not only a fun thing but a *work* fun thing. It is service. I am talking about volunteering. "What! Me work? I'm retired!" Of course you are. And you are entitled to do anything that brings you joy. But of all the things I know that can bring joy, volunteering heads the list. It opens up new worlds.

"Well, I might try it if I knew where to begin." That shows you are no sissy. "But I wouldn't know where to start." All right, may I offer a few suggestions?

If you love children, you could be a toy demonstrator to improve children's learning abilities through the use of selected toys and books. One man of eighty repairs and paints toys for children in an orphan home. Again, in working with children, you could feed those who are unable to feed themselves.

Other services you could perform include repairing books, helping in drug programs, raising money for college scholarships, reading to the blind, working in a mental hospital, etc. You say you do not know whether you could work in a mental hospital—you have no psychological training? Well, you could take patients for a walk, couldn't you? Or you could work in the hospital library, or sew costumes for the next show, or help to turn out the hospital weekly paper.

One person I know has sold beautiful clothes all her life. When she was asked to run a thrift shop in a home for the aged, she didn't know whether she could bear handling secondhand things. But she tried it. Selling is what she knew best. She likes it and she says: "I get lovely merchandise from lovely people. And the people who get them enjoy them so much. I come here three days a week. It's very rewarding."

Here we have a story of a bright-eyed Irishman who was fired with the idea that oldsters can do something for themselves. He got a small donated space in a mall, collected around him a dozen or so volunteers, and tries to help older people with their problems. There is no charge, and no questions asked about their politics or religion. He just helps them with whatever they need, whether it's glasses, hearing aids, dentures, or legal aid. (He has two low-fee lawyers who help with legal problems.) This interview service at the moment is drawing five hundred people to their weekly meeting and has given thousands of oldsters the "thirst and desire to manage their own affairs."

The government helps people with food stamps. But the poor widow often does not have a way to get to the government office to obtain authorization for the stamps. Nor does she have a way to get to the office that sells them, nor to the grocery to redeem the stamps. Some of the elderly need help with their shopping. If you are an older person yourself and can drive a car and are willing to help other persons with their problems, here is your chance. Volunteers are badly needed.

Or perhaps you are a good listener. Everyone wants someone to listen. Not the kind of listening in which a person is only waiting for a chance to step in and air his own troubles. But the kind that is accepting, patient, and willing to give the other person time. *Time*—that is a most important factor. Don't argue, just listen. Often people talk around things, and you think they will never get to the point. But eventually they do. Such listening is called creative listening, or listening with the third ear. Remember that when you are listening with interest to another person, you are telling him that you have respect for him. You have raised his ego image. Sometime you might need such listening yourself. Who knows?

If you don't want to work directly with people, stop at the nearest hospital and offer your services in the clerical division. If you don't like hospitals, go to the Red Cross. There's always a way to be useful.

Do you know what a VIP is? Usually this means a *very important person*. Well, in this case it *is* a very important person in a very special job, a *Volunteer In Probation*. A casual look at him would show an average person, but a closer look would reveal a person with character, a person of compassion—a person who feels with you deeply in his heart when you hurt—a person who wants to contribute a little of himself so that you may be helped.

This program was launched in Michigan by a young judge who was frustrated by the problems facing the lower courts. His aim was to prevent young lawbreakers, mostly charged with misdemeanors, from turning into habitual felons. There is a paid coordinator, but VIP is staffed mostly by volunteers who help guide the offender through his first critical brush with the law. They can use retired people. One such worker said: "Men who are in my position with so much leisure time on their hands should get into the volunteer program. They don't realize what pleasure it is to give pleasure to someone who has had very little happiness in his young life."

So, as you can see, I have just scratched the surface of possible places to serve. It would take a little looking into to decide just where your niche is. Of course it takes time, but what better use can you make of your time? You could do some volunteer work and still have enough time left over for just plain fun. If you use part of your leisure time this way, you will come to realize that it is a privilege to be able to contribute something worthwhile to help humanity. And if you don't get satisfaction, you can have your money back.

CHAPTER 10

School Bells
for the White-haired

> Old Age—To the unlearned, it is winter,
> To the learned, it is harvest time.
>
> —*Yiddish proverb*

A sissy quits learning. In high school he becomes a dropout. In marriage and on a job he does not realize what learning means, so he does not advance. At sixty-five, if he gets to be that old, he protests: "Who, me? Go to school? You must be crazy! Who needs it? What'll it do for me? Anyway, it's too late. I've earned my rest. Leave me be."

All right, all right. Nobody says you have to. You've earned your rest. Take it. But as to what learning can do for you, there is much to say. It can help you know what you are like so that you can live better with yourself. It can help you know what other people are like so that you can live better with *them*. You can find out what to do in this life—to change things or to leave things as they are. You will become more like what God—Oh, excuse me, you don't believe in God? I was going to say you will become more like what you were intended to be. Besides, learning can be fun! And think of the many friends you can gather on the way.

You act as if your life were nearly over. Maybe it is. Maybe not. Are you going to live the rest of your days in a vacuum? That can't be much fun. Life has a way of filling itself with *something*. Why not make it something worthwhile?

By the year 2000, more than half our population will be over fifty. People retire earlier and earlier, and that can only mean there will be a lot of living to be done after age fifty. Besides, there will be so many of us that the culture won't be so hung up on youth as it is now. Attitudes are bound to change.

Maybe you're lazy or just plain tired. You never did go for the education side of life, so why start now? Or perhaps you are still on the job. Sure, what you do on the job is important. But what you do with your life off the job is more important. You are going to have a lot of time on your hands, so why not prepare now? It won't be long before the four-day week takes over. That will give you even more extra time to manage. What will you do with it?

There are some people who don't agree with you that learning is a bore and a nuisance. Live and learn! Live and learn! That's their cry. It wouldn't surprise me at all if most industries would hold out the carrot of free, general education during job hours with job pay. Maybe you'll like it better then. "A mind is a terrible thing to waste"—a sign on a billboard. I believe it.

Learning is not something outside life. It is something within life waiting to be understood. Learning is a kind of big umbrella over everything else that happens to you. And it can help you whether you are buying a house, reading about heart trouble, studying your social security notices, or even trying to understand what's happening in Congress. Things are very different today from what they were when you were a youngster going to school. You need to know something about life so that when you look over the whole span of life you can understand its meaning. You can see the wholeness, even as the present blends into the future. If you don't think about the future, the chances are you won't have any.

We need to do something about changing the stereotypes. Let me tell a story about a Japanese student living with the family of a faculty member at a college. Coming down the stairs one evening, she saw the man of the house sitting in his favorite chair by the fireplace, reading. Suddenly she cried out, "Why, Harold, you're *middle-aged!*" He was wearing his new glasses for the first time. To her this was a symbol of age. Glasses meant age. It was as simple as that. Actually, he was only in his forties.

Most young people tend to think that way. If you're over thirty, you've had it. You can't be with it. As to forty, hey, man, that's an Age! You're practically in your grave. On the other hand, it's good that the young are taking a hard look at education. Sure, they say, if you're planning to be a doctor, lawyer, engineer, it's O.K. Otherwise it's for the birds.

What young people are saying is that learning is not relevant to living. They want to know how to live, *now*. Maybe it's time to take a good look at education in the schools, see what is being taught and how.

Maybe it's time to make education not only a preparation for living but a dimension of living. It also seems to me that the high schools and the colleges should not be for the young only, but should be places where the white-haired lady and the balding man can find stimulation. Why shouldn't the school bells ring for them too?

Of course there are other places where you can learn. Radio and television, for example. Educational television is a growing thing. Some of the programs are scheduled for early morning, but they're worth getting up for. Perhaps you want to learn a language—Spanish, for instance. You should see the eyes of a Mexican light up when you say even a few phrases in Spanish! Understanding a people's language is right next door to understanding a whole people. Only an Archie Bunker would have the arrogance to say, "Why can't everyone speak good, old American?"

Other places in which to learn are community centers, labor unions, churches, and museums. As far as museums are concerned, they are fascinating, but don't you wish that they didn't have such hard, polished floors, and that you could have a self-propelled wheelchair supplied to you, or at the very least a chair or a bench with a back for occasional resting? Express yourself to the museum authorities about these matters. Maybe they never thought of them.

If you are a person of low income, or in poor health, or possibly of a minority group, you are less likely to want to reach out to learn something new. In these cases, learning must reach out to you. Libraries have mobile units that will come to your area. Books for the blind not only are written in Braille but are also offered as "talking books" on phonograph records. (The library will lend you the machine.) Also there are books printed in large type for those who have poor vision. For news, there's the *New York Times* Large Type Weekly. For articles, the *Reader's Digest*. Learning is your right. Fight for it.

But the best place of all is the school. And truly, the school bell does ring for the elderly. Let me tell you about the Donovan Plan at the University of Kentucky, in Lexington, Kentucky. This plan was developed by the late President Emeritus Herman L. Donovan. He wanted to give older people a chance to have a meaningful experience, so he provided a fellowship—which means no fees—for men and women over sixty-five to study in the university, rubbing shoulders with the younger students.

This is a great opportunity and open to you if you have the physical stamina, emotional stability, good sensory reactions, a full measure of confidence, and if you can live without depending on any one else for your personal care.

The Donovan Fellowship is awarded for two semesters and a summer, and is renewable if you apply and are approved by the review committee. Living is off campus—in private homes or apartments. Good, inexpensive meals can be had in the student cafeteria. You don't even need a car. But you must be able to walk to and from classes.

What an opportunity! People from twenty states have gone to live in Lexington, located in the Blue Grass country. These individuals represent forty-four occupations. Educational background? This varies from the fourth grade in elementary school to a Ph.D. degree. You can take almost any subject. Or if you want to fit yourself for a second or third career, why not do it? For information, write to the Council on Aging, University of Kentucky, Lexington, Ky. 40506.

I must add that at the university there is a one-week summer course in creative writing. It is called the Writing Workshop for People Over Fifty-seven. It is excellent. I have attended it myself and can recommend it heartily. Two of its advantages are the fine quality of the teaching and the fact that it is limited to only fifty entrants.

Other colleges and educational centers are also offering courses for older people. In England there is The Third Age College. It boasts a registration of nearly one thousand persons. The movement for study among the elderly is spreading rapidly all over the United States. In Florida, for instance, the Palm Beach Junior College offers courses. Other places in the country are setting up programs like these.

Inquire, if you are interested, at the University of Denver in Denver, Colorado; Seattle Pacific College in Seattle, Washington; Ohio University in Athens, Ohio; Fairhaven College in Bellingham, Washington. And in New York, at Fordham University in the Bronx, New York City, and The City University of New York.

School bells are really ringing! Are they ringing for you? What have you got to lose but your boredom? A closing thought expressed by Dr. Edward Steiglitz: "If it is sensible for the child to make an effort to learn how to be an adult, then it is essential for the adult to learn how to be aged."

So go to it! And more power to you!

CHAPTER 11

Putting Old People Power to Work

> **The only thing necessary for the triumph of evil is for good men to do nothing.**
> —*Edmund Burke*

Politics in the United States is never a sure thing. There are always new issues and new ideas coming up for review. And who will be reviewing them? *We,* the people of the United States, where each adult has one vote. *We* will be deciding how the country is run; *we* are the jury who will decide what's what. Since the voting age was dropped to eighteen, much has been made over the new, young voter. But it is the older person who comes into the limelight as the key voter. Just think, over twenty million of us make up about a quarter of the total number of voters. Consider how much power we have, if we but take the trouble to use it!

In this technological society of ours, some people declare that elders should be disqualified. Why? Because, they say, knowledge does not accumulate with years; rather, it becomes outmoded. Therefore age is not an advantage. This is a lot of nonsense.

Consider: We oldsters have seen more changes perhaps than any other group in history. We remember the horse and buggy, the blacksmith shop, the horse-drawn streetcar (with its heating stove in the middle), the electric streetcar, the wood-burning stove to cook on, and later the coal-burning stove in the kitchen. We remember the old icebox, which became the modern refrigerator. We remember the first crystal-point radio with earphones, and the coming of television. We remember the oil lamp, then the gas lamp, then electric lighting for our homes. Moreover, we have been through two great wars and at least two lesser ones. We remember the first airplane flight across the ocean, and we have seen the first man land on the moon. We've been through something, what?

I am not one who believes that for all this the world owes us something. Rather, it is we who owe something to those who are coming after us, the young. I am appalled to hear anyone say: "What's the use? The world is doomed. We are living under a threat of total devastation—and I couldn't care less if the whole world went up in smoke with me when I die." What kind of thinking is this? People who have this attitude are sissies, pure and simple, or maybe not so pure and not so simple. In any case, sissies of the first water. I think we owe it to ourselves, to our fellowmen, and to God above all, to make of our lives the best thing possible.

Our country has just been through a time of acute distress. The series of shocking events called Watergate proves that we must get more and more interested in the way our country is run. No man can do it alone, but you and I, and many, many others, can help the country get straightened out again, if we remember our heritage and the Founding Fathers who set out to make a more perfect union, with liberty and justice for all.

After all, what does the word "politics" mean? The "poli" part refers to citizens; the word means the conduct of government of citizens. Unfortunately the word "politician," while it has the meaning of statesman, also has another, less flattering meaning. "Oh, he's a politician," you say, meaning he's a conniver, working mostly for public office and a chance to make a fast buck. But this is not necessarily so. One White House aide caught in the middle of the Watergate mess, when asked what advice he would give young men about politics, said, "Tell them to keep out of it."

I have a different opinion. I hope you have too. My idea is that the more good and honest people involve themselves with government, the better. You may say you are not educated enough. If you are educated enough to be on a jury, you are educated enough to judge what is happening in your country. And if you feel the need for further knowledge, get that learning we talked about before. Take a class in political science, or join a discussion group in a senior center. You have experience. You have wisdom. You have time. You should have the incentive to want to leave this world a better place than you found it. Many retirees, both men and women, work in government and enjoy it. It is exciting to be where the action is.

Let's assume that you think you may be of help in

getting better government. What to do? The most important single thing you can do is to get out there and vote. If you have something to say, say it in the polling booth. For you are part of the grass roots of our nation, and elections are most often won or lost right where you are, in the precincts. However, before you vote, it is necessary that you be registered to vote.

If you are not sure what to do or just where to go, get in touch with one of these three: the county election commission, the local council on aging, or the League of Women Voters. None of these root for any particular party, but they will get information for you on *all* candidates. The League of Women Voters will arrange transportation for you on Election Day. In addition, in most cities a pamphlet is put out on the issues and the candidates. Don't be afraid of being influenced for this or that candidate. The League's bylaws specifically state that it "shall not support or oppose any political party or candidate." The League also conducts informational programs on behalf of governmental issues.

As for voting, you can vote for any candidate, except in the primaries, when you're restricted to voting for the candidates of your party. From my experience, the best time to go to the polls is between 9 and 10 A.M. The voting machines are a bit scary. (Remember the old days when you marked your ballot with a blue pencil?) What you do now is get an identification slip from the registering clerk, and give it to the person in charge of the voting machine. The booth is open. To close it, pull the red handle to the right as far as it will go. Do not touch this handle again until you are ready to leave. If you need help of any kind, push the curtain apart with your hand and ask for it. *Take your time*—it can be a very confusing business. To vote for the candidate of your choice, push down the lever directly over his name. *Leave it down.* For a Yes or No question, do the same thing. Leave the lever down. Should you make a mistake, just push the lever back to where it was and press down the lever you want. It may not seem to you as if you were voting, because nothing seems to be recording. But pulling the red handle to the left as you leave the booth records your votes.

How do you know which person to vote for? Listen to the candidates on television. Read the papers. But best of all, if the one you prefer is already in office, look up his record. See how he voted in such and such a case, especially in regard to older people's problems. For instance, many legislatures have been struggling with the generic drug issue, that is, with whether a doctor should prescribe a drug by generic name, or whether he indicates a specific brand name. (Sometimes you *do* need a special brand.) For the most part, if you could buy a lesser-known brand, it costs less. For older people who spend much money on drugs this is an important issue. Should the druggist call the doctor for clarification? Should the druggist be required to have a display card explaining the issue? These are things that properly concern you.

The lawmakers want your opinion. They need your help. Here are some ways you can help:

Write to your congressmen and senators and tell them what you think. Put it in your own words. If they get a lot of letters alike, they'll think it's a pressure group. Write also to editors of newspapers. Learn about issues and men. And when you do, share what you learn with others.

Have a tea or a coffee in your home and invite people in to discuss issues and candidates.

If you have been a speaker and can address a group, this is your chance.

If you drive a car, take nondrivers to the polls and let them, too, exercise their privilege to vote.

If you can do leg work, do it. Volunteer to the campaign headquarters of your choice. They will assign you a job and be grateful for your help.

If you are unable to do the hard work, free another person to do it by taking care of her children for an afternoon or so.

Shut-ins can help with telephone assignments.

There is always something to do to help and it can be enjoyable. A spirit of camaraderie is established, which is really quite pleasant. However, don't go beyond your strength. And if you think this is a lot of work, it is. But it's important work, and it doesn't last forever.

In 1971 the White House Conference on Aging made some excellent recommendations. A few samples are given here:

Conferees suggested that education for political action should give instructions to help older persons understand procedures. These should be in good, plain English.

Work for legislation to eliminate age discrimination. If you need a job, or if you want to work, tackle this. The laws have already been made in some cases, but more vigorous enforcement is needed. If you agree that how old you are does not necessarily indicate how well you can perform, let that be known.

Conferees suggested that child care centers be staffed by elders. Children need the wisdom and experience of older people, and older folks need to hear and see children laugh and play. It's a mutual game of love.

They also recommended a flexible retirement arrangement rather than the present cutoff for all at a particular age.

These are only a few of the many recommendations, but this is neither the time nor the place to discuss them all with you. The important thing is to realize that if you want something, you have to go after it. It is the squeaky wheel that gets the grease. And if gentle ways of asking are not effective, get up on your hind legs and fight for what you want. Make a noise! There just is no other way. Your voice can be a very important one, and your influence is needed.

A group of activists come to mind. Headed by Margaret Kuhn, a woman of about seventy, these Gray Panthers are calling out to society that old people have rights. They are not to be humiliated, left on the shelf or the scrap heap. Together with four or five like-minded people, she started this group in Philadelphia in 1971, a group that has now grown to almost two thousand members, some of whom are young people. The "skip a generation" principle is active here. The young are beginning to realize that powerlessness affects them as well as the old, for both the young and the old are last to be hired and first to be fired. When Senator Edmund Muskie asked how the Gray Panthers came by its name, Margaret Kuhn answered: "The square name is the 'Consultation of Older and Younger Adults.' If we had used that, we might not have gotten where we are today." Here is a small, dedicated group exercising a power for social change. This is one illustration of what I have been talking about. Get your own political clout so that, among other things, you will be able to walk the streets at night without being afraid.

A saying that John Adams wrote in a letter is now inscribed on the mantel of the White House dining room. It reads:

> I Pray Heaven to Bestow
> THE BEST OF BLESSINGS ON
>   This House
> And All that shall hereafter Inhabit it.
> May none but Honest and Wise Men ever rule
>   under This Roof.

Old-people power can help this prayer come true.

CHAPTER 12

Some Who Made It— Famous and Unfamous

To me, old age is always fifteen years older than I am.—*Bernard M. Baruch*

It would seem that it is not how old you are but what you think of old age, particularly in yourself, that matters. So I am going to tell you about older people, some famous and others not so well known, who really didn't let age stand in their way when it came to getting something done. Many of them died with their boots on. Others worked until within a year of their death. The list could be enormous, but who has space or time for such a project? Anyway, I collected these:

Pablo Casals, 1876–1973, probably the world's foremost cellist, was of Spanish origin. Both conductor and composer, at the age of seventy-four he founded in France an annual festival of classical chamber music. At age eighty-seven he received the U.S. Presidential Medal of Freedom.

Cornelius McGillicuddy—Oh, you don't know him?

Perhaps you would recognize him better under the name *Connie Mack*, "The Grand Old Man of Baseball," who considered the first one hundred years the hardest, and who thought baseball was democracy in action. A moderate man—no tobacco, no drinking, no profanity—he lived to write his autobiography at age ninety (after scolding himself for writing in the *Saturday Evening Post* a series of articles entitled "Life Begins at 73." Such ideas he considered the "follies of youth"). For fifty years he managed the Philadelphia Athletics baseball team. His book, *My 66 Years in the Big Leagues*, reveals, through his Irish blue eyes, his integrity, his humanity, his orderliness. A superb American who knew how to live one day at a time.

W. Averell Harriman, born in 1891, American industrialist and financier, had a distinguished second career under several Democratic administrations, including that of Lyndon Johnson. He was a man of unswerving integrity, and at sixty-nine served in several federal posts. At seventy-eight he was called by C. L. Sulzberger "the world's most experienced negotiator," because of his work in the Vietnam peace talks. (Perhaps today he might have to relinquish that title to Henry Kissinger.)

Karl Jaspers, 1883–1969, a German philosopher and writer of important works in psychology, philosophy, and history, lived to be eighty-six though his health was always fragile. He took a chair of philosophy in Basel at age sixty-six, and from that vantage point spent the last twenty years of his life writing large historical works on various subjects, including German guilt and the atomic bomb.

Jacques Lipchitz, 1891–1973, was a sculptor whose art went in cycles, including cubism. This six-foot-tall, blue-eyed Lithuanian with light-brown (later gray) hair celebrated his seventieth birthday in a rather unusual way. He gave three hundred original plaster models of his sculpture to the American-Israel Cultural Foundation to be placed in the Jerusalem Museum of Art.

Archibald MacLeish, born in 1892, is an American poet, playwright, public official, and Pulitzer Prize winner. Graduated from Yale in 1915, he was the poetic weathervane for forty years. At sixty-nine he wrote his most important critical work, *Poetry and Experience.*

Grandma Moses, 1860–1961, America's best-known primitive painter, was the tenth child born to a farm couple. Her art started with embroidering pictures in yarn. When she was seventy-six her arthritis became so bad that she could not embroider anymore. Did she give up? Not this woman! She started painting. In 1940 at eighty she gave a one-man show (all right, you women libbers, a one-*woman* show) in New York City. This catapulted her into fame.

Henrietta Szold, 1860–1945, was an American Jewish leader who founded Hadassah and originated the Youth Aliyah projects, directed toward rescuing Jewish youth from Nazi Europe. At eighty she conducted a study of the occupational needs of young women and founded the Alice Seligsberg School for Girls in Jerusalem.

Pablo Picasso, 1881–1973. This Spanish-born painter, sculptor, and graphic artist was most prodigious. A revolutionary, he established the basis for abstract art. He was socially and politically aware of what was going on in the world. The supreme master of modern art, which had its beginnings in cubism, he worked until the last days of his life, being over ninety when he died.

Norman Thomas, 1884–1968, was born in Ohio, son and grandson of Presbyterian ministers. He worked in settlement houses, opposed American participation in war, and helped establish the American Civil Liberties Union. Strongly against Soviet Communism, he used his gift of oratory to oppose many public issues: the persistence of poverty and racism, for instance. During his last twenty years he was revered by many who could not go along with his political views. He remained amazingly active until his very last year.

Charlie Chaplin, a genius in pantomime, was born in 1889. He worked for many years acting and directing silent films and, later, talking films. At eighty-three he returned to the United States from England to be honored by major tributes in New York and Hollywood as one of the greatest figures in the movies.

Benjamin Franklin, 1706–1790. At sixty-two he became agent for Georgia, the next year for New Jersey, and the year following that, for Massachusetts. At sixty-seven he wrote the satire: "Rules by which a Great Empire may be reduced to a Small one." He served as a delegate to the Second Continental Congress at age sixty-nine. In 1776, when he helped with the drafting of our Declaration of Independence, he was seventy years old.

Amos Alonzo Stagg, 1862–1965, called the dean of

coaches, contributed much to the development of football rules and tactics, teaching the young to shoot square. He was a character builder for young men, a tough taskmaster with his teams. He received endless honorary degrees, and recognition from President Eisenhower and President Kennedy. Noted for his granitelike integrity that never compromised for victory, he set new standards for sportsmanship in college athletics. Being forced to retire at seventy, he said he was too young and had many years still to give to youth. So he continued to coach throughout his seventies and eighties.

Pearl Buck, American Nobel Prize winner, was born in 1892. A prolific writer, she dedicated her books and her personal activities to improving the relationship between Americans and Asians. *The Good Earth* (1931), a story of Chinese peasant life, brought her fame. At sixty-seven, she wrote *A Desert Incident,* which was produced in New York City. She died in 1973 at eighty years of age.

Giuseppe Verdi, 1813–1901, the most distinguished Italian opera composer, was commissioned by the government of Egypt to write an opera with an Egyptian subject. He came up with *Aida,* one of the most popular operas of all time. At age seventy-three he composed another remarkable opera, *Otello.* And four years later, the opera *Falstaff,* the miracle of his old age, was first performed in Milan when he was eighty.

Karl Menninger, Chief of Staff of the Menninger Clinic, a psychiatrist who did so much for mental illness, received so many awards—it's hard to give a picture of this man's work. At seventy-five, he wrote

The Crime of Punishment. This busy man has many leisure interests: horticulture, soil conservation, chess, music, American Indians, and wines. This proves it's the busy man who can do much.

Arthur Fiedler, whom everyone calls by his first name, was born in 1894, of Austrian-born parents. Asked if he likes rock and roll, he says: "A certain amount of it. It is completely American." He still directs the Boston Pops Orchestra (which mixes Bach with boogie-woogie), and speaks five languages—no, six (Polish, which he reserves to use when angry).

How can I stop? But stop I must, even though I must leave out *Arturo Toscanini, Artur Rubinstein, George Washington Carver, Thomas A. Edison, J. B. Priestley,* who at eighty says, "You're just the same inside," or *Chief Justice Earl Warren,* whose father said they were too poor to give him a middle name. This man, who died recently at eighty-three, gave this advice: "Have some interest in worthwhile things and apply yourself to them. Live moderately and have a family life." He was always happy to be with his children and grandchildren and said, "Their well-being is my chief concern." He had great respect for and understanding of the Constitution of the United States. He treated it as a living document rather than a piece of dead parchment. His is a life to study.

I just cannot leave out *Oliver Wendell Holmes, Jr.,* who was appointed to the Supreme Court when he was sixty-one and served until age ninety-one. Or *Michelangelo,* who carried out great architectural tasks during his seventies and eighties. But stop I must, otherwise I won't have room for some of the lesser-known people. Here are a few:

There is *Mother Terese*, an older Catholic nun and missionary, who worked not only in Calcutta, India, but in forty other countries. Her purpose is to teach those facing death how to die with dignity and in peace, through tender, loving care (TLC). Born in Yugoslavia of Albanian parents, she hopes to extend her work to Australia and even talks of opening a center for her work in the Bronx, New York City.

Eubie Blake, who appeared on the *Today* program, and whose parents were slaves, was born in 1883, is now ninety-one years old, and gives thirty to forty piano concerts a year (ragtime). "How do you stay young?" he was asked. "Well, I don't drink," he said.

Burt Mustin, who says retiring at eighty-eight is out of the question, he's having so much fun. He said: "Don't be afraid to try new things. I learned five jobs after I was fifty-seven."

Here's *Alvin Carlson*, in California, retired from his job as an industrial engineer, but he has never stopped working. He has two thousand old tools, which he considers valuable nineteenth-century antiques. He knows the blacksmith and woodworking trades. He says that when a house was built two hundred years ago, four craftsmen were represented: the carpenter, the joiner, the blacksmith, and the cabinetmaker. "When I awake in the morning," he says, "I feel blessed, and instead of wondering how I will fill my day, my thought is, 'How will I accomplish everything I want to do?' "

There are many, many others. The gray-haired astronaut *Donald Slayton*. And *Katharine Hepburn*, who at sixty-four is making a new movie. According to her: "They had to take us. That's all they had left."

But knowing her and her work, I find that hard to believe.

There's *Don Brand*, a freshman at sixty years of age. There is *Mr. Parker*, an eighty-three-year-old hollerer in a small town near Raleigh, North Carolina. There is *A. Philip Randolph*, past eighty. At seventy-four he was one of the organizers and leaders of the famous 1963 March on Washington.

Then there is *Mathilde Collins*, who, when she went for a physical checkup, was considered by the examining doctor to be sixty-two instead of nearly ninety.

There is *Mary Lull*, a physical fitness instructor at the Phoenix YMCA. Her measurements are 34-26-35, and she weighs 125 pounds. She has never worn a girdle and is seventy years old.

Here, too, I could go on and on. The Chinese have a saying, "There's one kind of rice, one thousand kinds of people." I agree. I have only this to add: Make your life good. Don't let anyone tell you that you belong on the shelf. That's the place for sissies, and surely you're not one. You have capacities, appetites, and you should have a zest for living.

So, get up and go! That's the only way I know to keep young, and when you have reached the fullness of your days, you will die young though your days are reckoned as many. After all, isn't that what living is all about?

CHAPTER 13

Saying "Yes" to Life

**We all want to and enjoy being loved. It enriches
our lives and gives us a feeling of happiness.**
—*Dr. Karen Horney*, Feminine Psychology

Do you realize that we are the first generation of
older people whose sheer numbers have grown to
such a size that we can be noticed? We cannot be
overlooked, nor can we be ignored. This is due partly
to science and partly to our own doggedness. We have
learned how to live longer. Now is the time to find out
for what?

When we look at the upcoming generation and see
them stirring to change what is bad in the world—
and many of them are honest in seeking better
values—we can have respect for them. They have no
experience of the old days but they do believe things
can be better. We, on the other hand, remember the
old days, the days before World War I, which we
innocently referred to as *the* World War, as though,
after this, there could be no other. We remember the
days of peace, when there was no atom bomb, no

MIRV, no threat that the world could in a few hours be destroyed.

I believe that we oldsters are here for a purpose, that our purpose is to give balance and steadiness to a world gone mad. Who better than old people, with the perspective and wisdom garnered from the years, can understand what is happening in the world and where we are going? But the young are the ones who are being listened to because they are making a noise; they are rebelling. And also because ours is a youth-centered culture. In old Japan, they used to respect the old people, and when someone wanted to know an older person's age, would ask, "How many years are you fortunate enough to have?" I suppose today's youngsters in Japan are pretty much like our own, more's the pity.

In a world where generations are separated, where old people have lost the respect of the young, where men are beginning to storm the cosmetic industry (I overheard one window cleaner say to another, "How do you like my $17 haircut?"), where unisex is not only a new word but a new concept, where abortion is generally approved, where the average home has its own bar and thus shows youth the way to alcoholism, where on a larger scale a Watergate is possible—in such a world, isn't there work for us?

I heard one older person say: "Thank God I have only a few more years left. I'll soon be out of this mess of violence, drugs, muggings, and such." This person is reneging on his responsibilities. Such a person is—need I say the word? or by now, do you and I know each other?

Yet do we have enough strength for the job? God help us if we don't. Indeed, God *will* help us if we give him a chance. But we have to make the connection. And the connection is made through prayer. Yes, I know you thought I was talking about helping other people in the world. True. But the best way to start is with yourself.

There is a time for self-sacrifice and a time for self-protection, where you have to stop living for someone else and live your own life. For God made you whole. Your integrity is precious to him. Don't let others break you up into little pieces.

The first thing to do is to accept yourself. This is the opening wedge in learning to accept others. More than that: love yourself. Then and only then can you love others. Love is the greatest medicine, the greatest method, the greatest leveler.

I like to think of love as a quality of inner joy. Happiness seems shallow by comparison. Deep contentedness is more what I am thinking about. In retirement you are freed for many things: you have the most precious gift of all: time. You can do as you please, more or less. You have the opportunity to get to know people in depth. Before, perhaps you had made many acquaintances but few friends.

Everyone needs someone to talk to. Can you be that someone? Is your face full of light because of your love shining through? Are people drawn to you to tell you their innermost thoughts? Do they make you feel needed? What a great need in us to be needed!

As we simplify our lives by shedding our possessions, we find that instead of collecting *things* we

could collect ways to serve people. Aging in itself is
not new. But how to act in an aging situation *is*.
Admittedly, society's attitude toward aging needs to
be changed. But who is society but you and me? I
cannot change you. The only person I can really
change is myself. So start with that. How? Let's start
by saying "Yes!" to life. Perhaps then we can help
others do the same. In this way, link by link, we will
try to keep all of us contented and full of grace.

Where shall we look for this love that we want to
share with others? Where, but within ourselves.
Within each of us is that spark of God which wants to
love others, even unlovable ones, and even when we
cannot always like them. We can look for "that of
God" in each person, as the Quakers say, and this
increases and expands as people feel our love reach-
ing out to them. In a Red Cross training session,
when we were learning about person-to-person relationships, we were advised, "Halo everyone you
meet!" Isn't that an excellent idea? Send out the
warmth of your endearing love in a golden circle (yes,
the color of love is gold) to touch all those coming
within its beams. Indeed, over the telephone, you can,
through your voice, reach people with love. I have
seen this work often in cases where people use the
telephone to call shut-ins and the aged, where the
sheer warm vibration of the voice is found cheering
and helpful.

Within us is that force, that God-given force, which
seems to cry out for expression. And if you don't find
it there, pray for its appearance. Ask God to make
room in your heart for compassion. Through prayer
we can be in touch with God at all times. So enlarge

the place of your dwelling. Don't build a neat little
fence around yourself so that another person cannot
reach you. And discourage other people from making
little fences about themselves. Such barricades are
often used by the old because they are lonely, but
they only serve to keep love out. Know that to love is
to forgive completely. Never mind the dirty hair, the
sniveling nose, the soiled clothes, the nasty comment,
the unloving small action directed against you. Pass
through them to the real person. Get inside, where
the lovingness of the other person really lives. You
will be surprised at what you find.

I have gotten much solace from my Bible, which I
came to know rather late in life, particularly when I
was fighting through that grim experience mentioned in the Foreword. It was a brain tumor and it
had to be removed. For quite a while I did not know
whether I would live or die. But as I lay there, hardly
able to breathe, I knew that my soul was bound in the
bundle of life, with God. "And the souls of thine
enemies, them shall he sling out, as out of the middle
of a sling." (I Sam. 25:29.)

I was sitting reading Psalm 118: "The LORD is on
my side; I will not fear: what can man do unto me?"
when I happened to glance at a newspaper cartoon.
This showed a poor old man reading a sign in the
window of a restaurant. The sign said, "Free sand-
wiches to the needy." He shuffled in and asked for a
sandwich. "Sure," said the countergirl, "but first you
must prove you are needy. I have to see your Social
Security card, your employment record, your citizen-
ship papers, your health certificate, and a letter from
your last employer; also a copy of your last year's

income tax, your high school diploma, your service record, and a $10 deposit which will be returned to you when all this is checked out." He did everything she asked. Then she said: "Thanks. You'll receive your sandwich in the mail in just a few days." Exaggerated and somewhat on the incredible side, isn't it? But that's what man can do to you.

You may well ask: "How, then, can I say 'Yes' to life when such folderol is possible, when I am sick, or maybe blind, or hungry, or perhaps all three; when I don't have enough money to go to a doctor, or buy over-the-counter drugs I need? How can I not reject people when they reject me, when they think I'm too old to talk to, when no one listens to me anymore?"

There are no easy answers. But will it help your condition if you let it breed hate? I say "No." With whatever strength there is left in you, get up and fight. One way is to count your blessings—they may be very few, but count them anyway, and say a prayer of thanksgiving for them. "I love the Lord, because he hath heard my voice and my prayers. Because he hath listened to me (when no one else would) therefore will I call upon him as long as I live."

In other words, begin to generate love. Soon your mood will become quiet, your words more soft. You will begin to attract people to you, since you no longer complain. People will sense a change in you and will respond to the goodness you have discovered in yourself. It's worth a try, isn't it? Instead of a horrid old age, you may find a new dimension, so that you can complete and round out your circle neatly and happily.

We have picked up the mirror and looked at ourselves hard and long. We have found out where in the world we are and where we would like to be. And we know our work is cut out for us—to become what we envision. Say to the world: "The worst thing you can do to me is to ignore me. I won't let you." Say it even to the clothes manufacturers who make dresses that zip in the back, never considering how painful it can be for the poor old lady crippled with arthritis. (Those manufacturers are missing a good bet. There must be a vast market in clothes for older people— with bright colors and suitable styles, and easy to get into.)

Even buses, trains, and planes are designed for the younger generation. But with our numbers increasing, there must come a change. Get the young to see that their energy and youth, if harnessed, can help solve the problems of aging. Remind them that they are thereby helping themselves. They will be old too, one day. It isn't true that all the young are uneducated, oversexed, and superspoiled. A good many are filled with love, but don't quite know how to express it.

Remember, above all, that the mainsprings of courage and strength lie within. Some material comforts are needed, but a great many won't be missed. We have to give them up and show a willingness to grow, to change, to be creative. A friend wrote me recently: "Old age is like climbing a hill, a high hill, each step of which becomes harder and harder, but when you come to the top, what a wonderful vista!" Dream that impossible dream, for nothing is impossible with God. Saying "Yes" to life helps that dream come true.

In closing I give you this prayer which some people have found helpful. I wrote it in 1973 to usher in the New Year.

IN THE END

O Lord, in the end make me
Humble, yet sure;
Tender, yet not weak;
Loving, yet not sentimental;
Believing, yet not foolish;
Wise, yet not impatient;
Strong, yet not overbearing;
Sensitive, yet not easily hurt.

Make me, Lord,
Forgiving, yet not patronizing;
Sure, yet not smug;
Warm, yet not impassioned;
True, yet not stilted;
Tolerant, yet not accepting evil.

And, Lord, I would be
Humorful, yet not derisive;
Joyous, yet understanding sorrow;
Confident, yet not complacent;
Mature, yet not old.

Lord, make me
Purposeful, yet open to Thy will;
Vigilant, yet not suspicious;
Modest, yet not withdrawn;
Peaceable, yet not forcing my peace upon others.

Lord, I would be
Courageous, yet not aggressive;
Simple, yet not strange to my fellows;
Orderly, yet not rigid;
Rooted, yet free.

O Lord, make me more
Godly, yet not pious;
Make me an
Instrument for Thy Good.

Thus will I become transformed,
So that in Thy good time,
I will become,
In The End,
That which Thou hast planned for me
In The Beginning.

Amen!

—Reprinted from Friends Journal, *Jan. 1, 1973.*
Copyright Friends Publishing Corporation.
Used by permission.

Suggested Reading List

Armour, Richard, *Going Like Sixty*. McGraw-Hill Book Co., Inc., 1974.

Arthur, Julietta K., *How to Help Older People*. J. B. Lippincott Company, 1954.

Baird, Janet H., *These Harvest Years*. (Essay Index Reprint Series.) Reprint of 1951 edition, Books for Libraries, Inc.

Blanchard, Fessenden, *Make the Most of Your Retirement*. Doubleday & Company, Inc., 1963.

Cabot, Natalie Harris, *You Can't Count on Dying*. Houghton Mifflin Company, 1961.

Call, Alice, *Toward Adulthood*. J. B. Lippincott Company, 1969.

Collins, Thomas, *Complete Guide to Retirement*. Prentice-Hall, Inc., 1972.

Cumming, Elaine, and Cumming, William H., *Growing Old: The Process of Disengagement*. Basic Books, Inc., Publishers, 1961.

Curtin, Sharon R., *Nobody Ever Died of Old Age*. Little, Brown & Company, 1973.

Donahue, Wilma, *Planning the Older Years*. University of Michigan Press, 1950.

Ellison, Jerome, *The Last Third of Life Club*. United Church Press, 1973.

Fried, Barbara, *The Middle-Age Crisis*. Harper & Row, Publishers, Inc., 1967.

Fritz, Dorothy Bertolet, *Growing Old Is a Family Affair*. John Knox Press, 1972.

Gorney, Sandra, and Cox, Claire, *After Forty*. Dial Press, Inc., 1973.

Hart, Mollie, *When Your Husband Retires*. Appleton-Century-Crofts, 1960.

Hendrickson, Andrew, *Manual for Planning Educational Programs for Older Adults*. Florida State University Press, 1973.

King, Frances, and Herzig, William F., *Golden Age Exercises*. Crown Publishers, Inc., 1968.

Lang, Gladys Engels, *Old Age in America*. Harper & Row, Publishers, Inc., 1974.

Lawton, George, *Aging Successfully*. Columbia University Press, 1946.

Legler, Henry, *How to Make the Rest of Your Life the Best of Your Life*. Simon & Schuster, Inc., 1969.

Lewis, Adele, and Bobroff, Edith, *From Kitchen to Career*. The Bobbs-Merrill Company, Inc., 1965.

Luce, Gay G., and Segal, Julius, *Sleep*. Pyramid Publications, 1972.

Margolius, Sidney, *Your Personal Guide to Successful Retirement*. Random House, Inc., 1969.

Osterbind, Carter C. (ed.), *Independent Living for Older People*. (Center for Gerontological Studies and Programs, Vol. 21.) University of Florida Press, 1972.

Pearce, Donald, *Dying in the Sun*. Charterhouse Books, Inc., 1974.

Peterson, Robert, *New Life Begins at Forty*. Pocket Books, Inc., 1969.

Puner, Morton, *To the Good Long Life*. Universe Books, 1974.

Russ, Lavinia, *High Old Time: or How to Enjoy Being a Woman Over Sixty*. Saturday Review Press, 1972.

Scott-Maxwell, Florida, *The Measure of My Days*. Alfred A. Knopf, Inc., 1968.

Smith, Bert Kruger, *Aging in America*. Beacon Press, Inc., 1973.

Smith, Elliot D., *Handbook of Aging*. Barnes & Noble, Inc., 1973.

Soule, George, *Longer Life*. The Viking Press, Inc., 1958.

Steincrohn, Peter J., *Forget Your Age*. Doubleday & Company, Inc., 1945.

————*Live Longer and Enjoy It*. Prentice-Hall, Inc., 1972.

Stern, Edith, and Ross, Mabel, *You and Your Aging Parents*. Harper & Row, Publishers, Inc., 1965.

Taylor, Florence M., *The Autumn Years: Insights and Reflections*. The Seabury Press, Inc., 1968.

Thurber, James, *The Middle-aged Man on the Flying Trapeze.* Grosset & Dunlap, Inc., 1960.

Winter, Ruth, *Ageless Aging.* Crown Publishers, Inc., 1973.

For lists of helpful government publications, write to United States Government Printing Office, Superintendent of Documents, Washington, D.C. 20402. Some are free, others cost very little.

For information about government-sponsored voluntary action programs, write to your State Office of Aging, or to ACTION, Washington, D.C. 20525. Dial ACTION's toll-free number, 1-800-424-8580, for information and ask for the number of the nearest ACTION phone in your area.

Index

Acceptance
  of death, 49
  of yourself and others, 108
Accountant, as an aid in tax
  matters, 56
ACTION, 117
Adams, John, 97
Advertising, sex in, 38
Aging process, 23, 32, 44, 71,
  109
Ailments, overcoming limita-
  tions of, 34
Anger, effect of, 30 f.
Arteries, hardening of, 32
Aspirin, 25
Auctioneer, 62

Balance
  in diet, 27
  in society, 107
Balance sheet, assets and lia-
  bilities, 52
Banking
  value of, 52
  booklet, 57
Baruch, Bernard M., 98
Bible quotations
  III John 2, 22
  Prov. 15:23, 17
  Prov. 27:1, 44
  Ps. 84:3, 60
  Ps. 118, 110
  I Sam. 25:29, 110
Blake, Eubie, 104

Blindness as a handicap, 31
Body cells
  description of, 23
  relation to mind, 29
Books
  braille, 87
  large type, 87
  talking, 87
Brain
  capabilities of, 20
  arteries of, 32
  functions of, 23
  tumor, 110
Buck, Pearl, 102
Buddy telephoning system, 65
Bundle of life, 110
Burke, Edmund, 90
Buying on time, 57

Cancer
  predisposition for, 22
  clinic, 72
Capacity for problem-solving,
  34
Car
  buying, 53
  driving, 31, 34
Career openings, 88
Carroll, Lewis, 29
Casals, Pablo, 98
Changes in life-style, 90 f.
Channels, spiritual, 35 f.
Chaplin, Charlie, 101
Checking accounts, free, 52

CHEER, 58
Child care centers, 96
Choices for leisure time, 77 ff.
Comfort, Dr. Alex, 46
Communication, difficulty of, 49
Community, choice of, 64
Companies, retiring from, 69
Condominium living, 63 f.
Conference on Aging
    Florida, 37
    Wash., D.C., 95 f.
Confidence
    in nursing home situation, 66
    in sex, 43
    in study, 87
Confrontation, each day's, 36
Contract, signing, 64
Control of self, 30
Cooking for yourself, 28
Cooperation as basis for group therapy, 34
Council on Aging, University of Kentucky, 88
Country, state of our, 91 f.
Courage
    in accepting aids, 66 ff., 112 f.
    display of, 67 f.
    mainsprings of, 112
Creative writing course, 88
Creator as helper, 34
Credit cards, 52 f.
Cresthaven Villas, 63 f.
Cripples who overcame, 34
Crisis Line, 73
Crutch, temporary use of, 66 f.
Cycle of life, 44 f.

Dancing, square and folk, 78
Death
    Charles Frohman's concept of, 45

fear of, 46, 50
point of, 49 f.
Declaration of independence, personal, 19
Depression
    in nursing home, 32
    in terminal illness, 49
Developers, condominium, 63
Diet, 26 ff.
Dignity
    in accepting aids, 26, 67
    in death, 49
Discipline
    in buying, 53
    in sex, 38 f.
Discussion groups, 79
Doctor
    checkup by, 24
    limitations set by, 18
    prescriptions from, 94
Dollar inflation, 51 f.
Donovan, Herman L., plan, 87
Dress manufacturers, opportunity of, 112

Education
    for death, 47
    fun of, 84 ff.
Editors, writing to, 95
Ego image
    one's own, 18
    raising the, 81
Elimination, bodily, 24
Emotional health, 33
Emotions
    incapacity to understand death, 44
    in relation to body, 29 f.
Employment, age discrimination in, 69 f.
Exercise, physical, 23 f.
Exhaustion, dying of, 28
Eye bank, 48

Fabric of life, 47
Fact sheet when selling house, 61 f.
Faculties, mental and emotional, 33
Faith, as basic element, 33
Faith in action, 45
Family Service, 57
Famous people, 98
Fear
  as accident cause, 25
  of death, 44, 50
Fearfulness, as negative reaction, 30
Fees, mental health treatment, 33
Feelings, mind controlling, 30 f.
Fellowship, inspiration of group, 35
Fellowship Community, 21
Fénelon, 49 f., 76
Fiddler on the Roof, 79
Fiedler, Arthur, 103
Finances, handling of, 51 ff.
Food
  emotional need for, 30
  shopping for, 54 f.
Food stamps, 57 f., 80 f.
Foster Grandparents program, 73
Franklin, Benjamin, 101
"Freezing" as negative behavior, 30
Friendship as a way of life, 50
Friends Journal, 36, 114
Future
  concern with, 45
  quality of your work in, 75

Gadgets, useless, 53
Games, 77
Generic drug issue, 94

God
  belief in, 33 f.
  concept of humans, 108
  creation, 39
  pattern, 35 f.
  prayer to, 113
  reason for keeping you going, 21
Government
  and aging, 19
  better, 92 f.
Gray Panthers, 96
Great Books discussion groups, 79
Green Thumb project, 74
Group therapy as healing agent, 34
Gunther, John, 46

Habits, changing, 24
Handicaps, overcoming, 33 f.
Harriman, W. Averell, 99
Hate
  breeding, 111
  flushing out, 35 f.
Hazards, avoidance of, 25
Health, physical, 22 ff.
Health Clinic, 65
Health
  mental and spiritual, 29 ff.
  principles of, 23 ff.
Heart failure, 22
Hepburn, Katharine, 104
Heritage, remembering one's, 92
Hillel, Rabbi, 76
Hershfield, Harry, 22
Hobbies, development of, 71
Holmes, Oliver Wendell, Jr., 103
Home for aged, work plan, 71 f.
Home Nursing Service, 58

Horney, Karen, 106
House, choosing a new, 64 ff.
Housing, 60 ff.
Hungry man story, 110 f.
Husbands, retirement problems of, 71

Identification number, 55
Income, fixed, 53
   low, 86
Income taxes, 55
Inflation, effects of, 51 f., 60
Insecurity in the streets, 65
Inspiration of fellowship, 35
Integrity, preciousness of, 108
Interest, banking, 52
Internal Revenue Service, 55
Insurance, a hobby as, 71

Jaspers, Karl, 99
Joy
   in business of living, 50
   in leisure, 79
   in work, 75
   of sex, 39
   quality of inner, 108
Junk foods, 54

Kentucky, University of, program for older people, 87 f.
Kidneys, wearing out of, 22
Knees, locked, 31
"Knowing" (sex relationship), 39
Kübler-Ross, Dr. Elisabeth, 49
Kuhn, Margaret, 96

Labor Department and rehiring, 69 f.
Languages, learning, 86
Last third of life, 77
Lawyer, need for, 56

League of Women Voters, 93
Learning
   as an opportunity, 87
   in later years, 19 f., 83 ff.
Ledger, organizational, 48 ff.
Leisure, use of, 76 ff.
Levenson, Sam, 26 f.
Liabilities, listing of, 49, 52
Library, mobile units, 86
Life, confrontation of, 50
Lift Line, transportation for elderly, 58
Lipchitz, Jacques, 100
Listening, creative, 81
Loneliness
   barrier of, 34
   number one killer, 65
Little theater, 78 f.
Love
   as an ingredient, 28
   as joy, 108
   channel of, 35
   color of, 109
   first taste of, 27
   in the young, 112
   the greatest medicine, 108
   to be generated, 111

Mack, Connie, 98 f.
MacLeish, Archibald, 100
Maintenance-free living, 64
Marquis, Donald R. P., 34
Meals-on-wheels, 58
Medicaid, 58
Medicare, 58
Medicine
   greatest, 108
   prescribed, 24
Memories of bygone days, 91
Menninger, Karl, 102 f.
Menopause, 37 f.
   sex after, 42 f.
Mental health, 29 ff.

Mental hospital, work in, 80
Michelangelo, 103
Middle age, concept of, 85
Mind
  activities of, 79
  losing the, 29 f.
Minerals in diet, 27 f.
Miracles, expectation of, 35
Money
  use of, 51 ff.
  wasting, 57
  working for, 70
Mortgage
  importance of, 63
  paid-up, 60
Moses, Grandma, 100
Moving, 60 ff.

Nash, Ogden, 51
Nature, 33
Need, the great, 108
Nervous system, 29 f.
News, keeping abreast of, 31
New York Times, Large Type
  Weekly, 87
Nursing, as infants, 26
Nursing home
  choosing of, 65 f.
  experience in, 31 f.

Old people power, 90 ff., 96 f.
Order, putting affairs in, 48
Organic changes, 32
Organizations and housing,
  67 f.
Overcoming
  death, 50
  handicaps, 34

Paralysis, possible cause of, 30
Patients, in nursing home, 31 f.
Pattern of living, 24
Peace Corps, 74

Picasso, Pablo, 100 f.
Pneumonia, attitude toward,
  31
Political record, 94
Politics, 90 ff.
Poor (financially), 57
Positive behavior, 30 f.
Possessions, shedding of, 62,
  64 f.
Prayer, 108, 113
Pride, false, 31
Priestley, J. B., 103
Proteins, 27 f.
Psychological changes, 32 f.
Purpose of aging, 106 f.

Quaker Meeting, 34

Radio, 53, 86
Randolph, A. Philip, 105
Reacher, wooden, 25
Reader's Digest, large type edition, 87
Recreation, as a part of life, 77
Red Cross
  recreation worker, 72
  training session, 109
  volunteering for, 81
Religion
  and sex, 42
  as aid to self-understanding,
    33
Renewal, day of, 36
Resources slipping away,
  51 f.
Retired people as volunteers,
  81 f.
Retirement
  flexible arrangement, 96
  home, 65 f.
  shock of, 70
RSVP, 73 f.

Schooling, opportunities for, 83 ff.
Schumacher, Dr. Sallie, 37
Science, donation of body to, 48
SCORE, 74
Security through faith, 33 f.
Self-pity, 18, 30
Senility, 32 f.
Senior citizens, 17, 43, 52, 70, 78
Septuagenarian, 41
Service for others, 79 f.
Sewing
  costumes, 80
  market for, 71
Sex, 37 ff.
Shelf, getting put on, 72
Shut-ins
  at work, 95
  telephoning, 109
Silbiger, Dr. Norbert, 78 f.
Silence, sitting in, 36, 49
Smith, William C., 75
Social Security, 41, 58
  Supplement, 58
Society
  attitude toward aging, 109
  attitude toward sex, 42 f.
  technological, 90 f.
Sorrow in the world, 36
Spirit, people of, 32
Spotlight off ourselves, 34
Springs of the soul, 36
Stagg, Amos Alonzo, 101 f.
Steiglitz, Dr. Edward, 88 f.
Stock market, 54
Strehler, Dr. Bernard, 46
Subconscious, 22, 33
Supermarket, 54
Suspiciousness, 30
Sustenance, each day's, 36
Szold, Henrietta, 100

Teacher, retired, 70, 77
Teen-agers and sex, 43
Television, 86
Terese, Mother, 104
Terminal illness, 49
"That of God," 109
Thomas, Norman, 101
Thrift, 51
Time, use of, 22 f., 45, 65, 77 81 f., 108
Transportation
  to meals, 58
  to polls, 93
Typewriter, for handicapped, 34

Ulcers, 25
Umbrella
  full of holes, 51
  learning as overall, 85
Uselessness, feeling of, 30

Vacuum, life in a, 84
Values, new set of, 19
Verdi, Giuseppe, 102
Vertical line toward God, 35
Vestibule of death, 50
VIP, 81 f.
Visiting Nurse, 66
VISTA, 74
Voice, effect of warm, 109
Volunteers, 73 f., 79 ff., 117
Voting, importance of, 93 f.

Walking aids, 31 f., 66 f.
Wall Street, 54
Warren, Chief Justice Earl, 103
Watergate, 91 f.
West Palm Beach, 64
White House
  Conference on Aging, 95 f.
  mantel prayer, 97

Wheelchair, 31, 66 f., 86
Will, importance of making, 48
Withdrawal, emotional, 30
Work, 69 ff., 75
World, our place in, 17 f.
Writing
  to lawmakers, 94 f.
  workshop, 88

"Yes!" to life, 109, 111, 113
Yesterdays, our, 26
Yiddish proverb, 83
Youth
  and sex, 38
  preparing for aging, 70
  rubbing shoulders with, 87
  truth about, 112